CW00951278

THE SWEDISH ARMY IN THE GREAT NORTHERN WAR 1700–21

Organisation, Equipment, Campaigns and Uniforms

Lars Ericson Wolke

'This is the Century of the Soldier', Falvio Testir, Poet, 1641

Helion & Company

The Commissioning Editor would like to thank Boris Megorsky and Sergey Shamenkov for their generous help and advice during the creation of this book.

Helion & Company Limited
Unit 8 Amherst Business Centre
Budbrooke Road
Warwick
CV34 5WE
England
Tel. 01926 499 619
Fax 0121 711 4075
Email: info@helion.co.uk
Website: www.helion.co.uk
Twitter: @helionbooks
Visit our blog at http://blog.helion.co.uk/

Published by Helion & Company 2018
Designed and typeset by Serena Jones
Cover designed by Paul Hewitt, Battlefield Design (www.battlefield-design.co.uk)
Printed by Henry Ling Limited, Dorchester, Dorset

Text © Lars Ericson Wolke 2018
Colour images as individually credited. Black and white Images open source unless otherwise credited
Maps drawn by Derek Stone © Helion & Company 2018

Cover: The Swedish Guards storm the Russian earthworks at Narva, 30 November 1700. Illustration by Steve Noon © Helion & Company 2018

Every reasonable effort has been made to trace copyright holders and to obtain their permission for the use of copyright material. The author and publisher apologise for any errors or omissions in this work, and would be grateful if notified of any corrections that should be incorporated in future reprints or editions of this book.

ISBN 978-1-912390-18-2

British Library Cataloguing-in-Publication Data.
A catalogue record for this book is available from the British Library.

All rights reserved. No part of this publication may be reproduced, stored in a retrieval system, or transmitted, in any form, or by any means, electronic, mechanical, photocopying, recording or otherwise, without the express written consent of Helion & Company Limited.

For details of other military history titles published by Helion & Company Limited, contact the above address, or visit our website: http://www.helion.co.uk

We always welcome receiving book proposals from prospective authors.

Contents

List of Illustrations & Maps

Introduction

The Great Northern War (1700–21) was not only one of the most protracted wars that Sweden has ever fought, it was also the most costly, measured in losses of human lives. When the war started Sweden was a great power which ruled much of the Baltic Sea region; when the war ended this Swedish empire had fallen into pieces, after a long death struggle. Instead Russia was the new great power of the region.

The Swedish era of greatness began in 1561, when the city of Reval (Tallinn) and the northern parts of Estonia put themselves under the Swedish crown, in order to avoid being taken by Russia. But in Finland, then the eastern part of the Swedish realm, the year 1617 is regarded as the first year of the Swedish empire. It was the year when the peace treaty with Russia was signed at Stolbova, a peace that meant that Russia lost all her coastline along the Baltic Sea and was pressed eastwards. In 1710 Russian troops conquered most of Sweden's possessions along the eastern shore of the Baltic Sea, although it was not until the peace treaty at Nystad that these territories formally became Russian.

Since 1561 and during the 17th century Sweden fought four wars with Poland, five with Denmark–Norway and three with Russia, besides participating in the Thirty Years' War between 1630 and 1648. Some of the first of these wars resulted in victories, some in defeats, but from 1617 and onwards every war resulted in armistices or peace treaties that were favourable for Sweden. This long series of victories was broken only twice, by minor backlashes. The first by the peace with Denmark 1660 when Trondheim County in Norway and the island of Bornholm were returned to Denmark after only two years in Swedish possession, and the second by the peace with Brandenburg (Prussia) in 1679, when parts of Sweden's Hinterpommern were lost.

This meant that the Great Northern War began when Sweden's era of greatness culminated and ended with the same empire's collapse. It explains why these 21 years of war, of which 18 were with Charles XII as the King, for generations have attracted interest from scholars, writers and the public. Much of that interest has been focused on the King himself, on Charles XII, who has both been worshiped as a national hero, and also been regarded as the one who led Sweden and its people into death and destruction.

Charles XII's time on the throne (1697–1718) used to be knitted together with the reigns of his father Charles XI (1660–99) and grandfather Charles X Gustavus (1654–60), as the Carolean epoch in Swedish history. The first and the last of these three Carolean kings led the country in war, both aggression and defensive wars, while the second one above all fought a costly war against Denmark, when Sweden with a small margin managed to keep the former Danish provinces once conquered in 1645 and 1658. But Charles XI also spent 20 years of peace to build and reorganise the country and above all its army and navy. The modernisation of the army and the navy were more or less finished when the war broke out in 1700. That is why the history of the military reforms of Charles XI is indispensable for everyone who wants to understand the function of the Swedish army during the following two decades of war.

For decades a vast amount of research has been accumulated about different aspects of the Swedish armed forces during the Carolean age, and especially the army during the Great Northern War. In this book I will try to present the present knowledge out of my own and others' research, and thus describe and discuss the Carolean army during the Great Northern War.

1. Charles XII in 1707, by Johann David Schwarz. Royal Armoury (Livrustkammaren), Stockholm

Since the 13th century, and possibly some decades before that, Finland was an integrated part of the Swedish realm, all the way until 1809. So when I talk about Sweden it always includes Finland. At some times during the period before 1809 they used to talk about the western (today's Sweden) and eastern (Finland) parts of the realm. But from a legal point of view Finland was an integrated part of Sweden. Sometime the term the "Finnish army" was used, and that meant those army units that were operating in or from Finland, or sometimes had been recruited in the eastern part of the realm. In similar ways the terms the Northern army, the Western army or the Scanian army were sometimes used to describe forces that were operating in a specific region or direction. But there was no Finnish army separated from the Swedish. The other provinces in the Baltic region and northern Germany had a different form of formal connection to Sweden, but none of them were totally integrated in the way the landscapes and counties of Sweden and Finland were.

During the early 17th century and also in modern literature several place names have been changed, especially the case in Estonia and Latvia. That is why I use the contemporary names (often German ones), and in parentheses give the present name (for instance: Reval – Tallinn).

A problem for anyone who writes about the Great Northern War is that Sweden until 1753 used the Julian calendar, and then began to use the Gregorian. Thus for a long time Sweden's calendar was 10 days after the Continental one (now also used by Sweden). But it should be more complicated. In 1700 Charles XII ordered the removal of one day, the leap day, of that year. Suddenly Sweden had a calendar of her own. But in 1712 a new reform added two leap days in order to make a return to the Julian calendar. So February 1712 had 30 days in Sweden. In much of modern Swedish literature the Julian calendar is used, and so also in this book, in order to correspond with the main bulk of the literature.

As a consequence the battle at Düna outside Riga was fought on 9 July 1701 in Swedish contemporary and modern literature, but on 19 July in Saxon contemporary sources or modern German or Polish literature. Anyone who uses Russian sources or literature will find that the battle took place on 8 July.

For a long time the fundamental question for most historians was, why did the Swedish empire collapse at the end of the Great Northern War? But during recent decades the focus of research has been towards another question: how could the Swedish empire last for such a long time, and even 12 years after the disaster at Poltava?

This book will try to give answers to these big and complicated questions, by describing how the Swedish army was recruited, organised, trained, equipped and, not least, behaved tactically on the battlefield.

1

The Strategic Situation in the Baltic Sea Region in the Year 1699

Sweden in 1699 can be described as a maritime empire. This Swedish Baltic empire can be described as built around a central axis, an axis that went from the Lake Mälaren in the west, over Stockholm and Stockholm's archipelago further eastwards over the Åland islands, Åbo in Finland and along Finland's southern archipelago all the way to Viborg (Finnish: Viipuri; Russian: Vyborg) in the most eastern part of the Gulf of Finland.

Around this axis a number of landmasses had been tied during the 16th and 17th centuries when the empire grew bigger and bigger. This Swedish-Finnish empire was held together by water and sea lines of communication, and that fundamental structure was not changed when new Estonian, Ingrian, Latvian, Danish, Norwegian or German territories were incorporated into the empire. In fact, the opposite: the more the Swedish Baltic empire expanded, the more its nature as a seaborne empire was stressed.

One should also remember that before the arrival of the railroads in the mid 19th century, it was the waterways, river, lakes or seas that were the most important lines of communication. Water connected landmasses, while large areas of forests (very common in Sweden) separated them.

With this perspective it is very natural that the capital Stockholm, when it was founded in the mid 13th century, was placed just where Lake Mälaren met the Baltic Sea, but also where an important road went from southern Sweden further up to the provinces north of Stockholm. The city came to be in the very centre of the growing realm, just in between its Swedish and Finnish parts. It was not until Finland was lost to Russia after the war 1808–09 that Stockholm became a border town, but still in the early 18th century the city was situated in the very centre of the Swedish Baltic Empire.

It is important to understand that also Denmark, later the Danish-Norwegian Kingdom was built in a similar way. The capital Copenhagen was founded in the late 12th century in the very centre of Denmark of that time, between the Danish islands and the Danish lands of Scania, Halland and Blekinge. When Norway in the 16th century was forged to the Danish

2. Frederik IV of Schleswig-Holstein-Gottorp. Married to Charles' sister Hedvig Sophia, he was killed at Kliszów in 1702. By David Klöcker von Ehrenstrahl.

Kingdom, the sea lines from Copenhagen to southern Norway were simply added to the fundamental structure of that kingdom. Disaster came in 1645 and then 1658, when the peace treaties in Brömsebro and Roskilde meant that eastern Denmark, east of Öresund, became southern Sweden. In that way, 1658 especially was a Danish equivalent to Sweden's 1809 disaster. The court at Copenhagen could not accept that development, and in the 1670s a costly but failed attempt was made to reconquer the lost lands east of Öresund. It is that revanchism that explains Denmark's participation in the three-power alliance against Sweden in 1700. But added to that reason for a Swedish–Danish animosity came the problem of Holstein-Gottorp, the neighbour just south of Denmark.

Denmark feared, not without reason, that Sweden would encircle her by the acquisition of new provinces in northern Germany in 1648 and an alliance with Holstein-Gottorp. The Duchy had already been used as a back door to Denmark by invading Swedish armies in 1643 and 1657, and now its Duke Frederik IV was a cousin of King Charles XII of Sweden, and in 1698 had also married Charles' sister Hedvig Sofia. This of course resulted in stronger ties between Sweden and Holstein-Gottorp. How this development was regarded in Copenhagen is not difficult to understand.

In the Commonwealth of Poland-Lithuania the ambition was not only to get revenge for the terribly costly Swedish invasion in 1655–60 (the "Great Deluge"). The Poles also wanted to get back their former influence in Livonia (northern Latvia and southern Estonia), an influence that had been lost when Swedish forces in 1621 conquered Riga and took it from Poland. When in 1697 the Kurfürst of Saxony, Friedrich August I (through political intrigues) also became King August II of Poland and Grand Duke of Lithuania, the Commonwealth gained more strength. Thus a war against Sweden no longer seemed hopeless.

Sweden's third neighbour, Russia, had been excluded from all her coastlines along the Baltic Sea in the peace treaty at Stolbova in 1617. The whole province of Ingria (Ingermanland) and large parts of Karelia were lost to Sweden, who then expanded her empire east of Finland and Estonia. The whole of the river Neva between Lake Ladoga and the Gulf of Finland became a part of Sweden, and Ladoga became a partly Swedish and partly Russian lake. With the exception of a war in the late 1650s the rest of the 17th century had been relatively peaceful between Sweden and Russia. But that did not mean that Russia had forgotten her ambitions to once again reach the Baltic Sea, far from it. However, for many years Moscow regarded Poland-

Lithuania as Russia's most dangerous enemy and in that strategic situation Sweden could even be used as a threat against Poland in the north and the west. That is why Russia even financially supported Sweden's participation in the Thirty Years' War, since the Swedes fought the Emperor in Vienna, one of Poland's allies. In the deep south Russia was also engaged in a power struggle with the Ottoman empire and the Khan of Crimea (an ally of the Sultan in Constantinople) as well as with Persia.

But when in 1682 Peter Romanov became Tsar of Russia, together with his half-brother and co-regent Ivan V, the ambition to reach the Baltic Sea once again became a priority goal in Russian politics. This became more evident when Peter, step by step, reached the full power when he arrested his half-sister Sofia in 1689, his mother Natalia Naryshkina died in 1694 and his half-brother and co-regent Ivan V passed away in 1696.

Peter had three strategic goals: to reach the Baltic and the Black seas, and also expand towards the south in the Caucasus as well as on the Caspian Sea. The way to do this was to modernise and expand the Russian army, to create a Russian navy (founded as late as in 1696) and to modernise the civil service. Peter was convinced that only a modernised or westernised Russia could reach the position as an important European great power. But Russia could not advance in all directions at the same time, and it was not until after the Great Northern War, in 1722, that Peter launched a campaign against Persia. But his first and most important goal was to reach the Baltic Sea.

Thus a situation had developed with three revanchist enemies of Sweden forming an alliance in 1699 and waiting for the best moment to attack. When the old King Charles XI died in 1697 and his young son became the new ruler as Charles XII, at the age of 15, it was thought in Moscow, Warsaw, Dresden and Copenhagen that the right moment had arrived. After preparations, the war broke out in the year 1700.

2

The Organisation of the Swedish Armed Forces

In the late 17th century the Swedish army had for a long time had severe difficulties financing a sufficient number of well-trained units. When the Swedish empire during the 16th and 17th centuries grew along the coastlines of the Baltic Sea, it also meant that the demand grew for army and naval forces in order to defend it against revanchist neighbours. Thus the problem of how to secure the financing of the armed forces became increasingly acute.

In the 1540s a professional army of 15,000 men was organised, a number that grew during the following years. The next building block was the decision in 1619 by Gustavus Adolphus that all men from the age of 15 should be ready for military service if they were called out. Every third or fourth year conscription meetings were held in every parish, where one out of 10 of the men were taken to the army or the navy. This was the way to recruit national units to the armed forces between the years 1620 and 1680, and resulted in large numbers of relatively cheap soldiers. But the other side of the coin was of course the dramatically large casualties. During the last century of Sweden's era of greatness, from 1621 to 1721, about every third grown-up man in Sweden died in the service of the army or the navy, either in battle or as a result of starvation, illnesses or frostbite. With casualties of that size, the demand for foreign mercenaries grew to meet the never-ending demands for new soldiers.

When he landed in northern Germany in 1630 to enter the Thirty Years' War, Gustavus Adolphus had 14,000 men with him, most of them Swedes. Two years later, in the summer 1632, Gustavus Adolphus commanded more than 150,000 men, almost 90 percent of them Germans, but also large numbers of Scots, Englishmen, Irish and other nationalities. However, the culmination for the large armies of mercenaries reached its peak in the 1640s, when financial resources had been overextended as far as was possible.

But the decisive turning point did not come for another three decades, during the war with Denmark in 1675–79, when an invading Danish army was very close to reconquering Scania from Sweden. Only with large human and economic sacrifices did Charles XI and his military advisors manage to save the new border along Öresund. After that war the big question was how to prevent that anything like that happening again, and to make Scania and the other former Danish and Norwegian provinces – Halland, Blekinge, Bohuslän, Jämtland, Härjedalen, Gotland and Ösel – safe for Sweden?

The answer demanded a reformation of the armed forces. After a decision by the parliament in 1682 an allotment system, or "the certain maintenance of soldiers" was introduced step by step during the 1680s and 1690s. Formal contracts were signed between the Crown and the farmers and nobility in each province or county. At the end the construction of the new system was finished. Thus the Carolean allotment system was created, with just above 40,000 soldiers in the army and sailors in the navy.

The fundamental idea with the new system was that every province or county, in peace as well as in war, should raise and maintain one infantry regiment of 1,200 men. At least two, but sometimes up to 12 farms (depending on their size) formed a "rote" that would recruit one soldier and provide him with a croft and a piece of land for him and his family to live upon. The infantry regiment was divided into eight companies of 150 men each.

The sailors in the navy were recruited and maintained in the same way, and organised in naval or sailors' companies. Cavalry regiments were also organised in the different provinces or counties, but here one cavalry man and his horse were raised by wealthier farmers that were also given crofts and a piece of land. In exchange these farmers, called *rusthållare*, were exempted froim tax. Every allotted cavalry regiment consisted of 1,000 men.

In this way the army and navy gained volunteer soldiers and sailors – looking for the possibility to be able to use a croft and cultivated land that they never could afford to buy on their own, while the maintenance was relatively cheap for the Crown. The farmers provided the land and the soldiers worked on their crofts in order to support themselves and their families. This was a revolution since most, if not all, of the Swedish national soldiers since 1619 had been conscripted.

Every officer received a farm or a residence (*boställe*) equivalent to his military rank, and when he was promoted he and his family moved on to a larger residence with more land. Only minor salaries in cash were given, the main income for both officers and men coming from what they produced on their residences and crofts. If a soldier's croft land was of worse quality that those of his comrades, the farmers were obliged to provide him with extra seed, food and other goods as an equalisation.

The most important advantage for the farmers was that once they had recruited a soldier and given him his croft, their own sons were safe, for the old and much-hated conscription system had taken so many lives from Swedish farmers.

At the base of the command structure were the corporals, who commanded and exercised 10–25 soldiers living close to the corporal's residence. He gave them their first, basic military training, but also kept on eye on the men in their everyday life at home on their crofts. But all NCOs and officers, from the corporal up to the colonel of the regiment, were not only commanders of their men but were also obliged to, if needed, defend the interests of the soldiers against the farmers who had recruited them and provided them with their croft.

All officers, NCOs and soldiers were living spread out in the province or county where the regiment was recruited. While smaller groups of men were trained by their corporals, the companies met at their captain's residence for exercises and drill was also performed outside the church every Sunday. The whole regiment was exercised, sometimes together with other regiments in larger manoeuvres, at the regiment's exercise field. Here the regiment was trained for 3–4 summer weeks, ending in a midsummer party where the civilian population in the area took part. After that everyone went home to his officer's residence or soldier's croft. This was the annual routine of the allotment system in peacetime. In war the regiment was of course mobilised and sent away into the field with the army.

The Carolean allotment system was described in 1694, in fancy words, by the English diplomat John Robinson, who for almost a quarter of a century worked in Stockholm. He concluded about the discipline and good behaviour of the soldiers: "the good Effect of the Officers constant Residence, upon their respective Charges, appears in the quiet and peaceable Behaviour of the Soldiers, who have not hitherto, broke out neither into any Enormities, nor given the common People any great occasion of complaint."

This system was based upon one important condition: the expansion of the Swedish empire was finished and now Sweden should concentrate upon defending the established borders. No more wars for conquest, the new Carolean army and navy were created to be strategically defensive.

3

The Swedish Army in the Year 1700

The Swedish armed forces consisted at the outbreak of the war in the year 1700 of 58 larger or smaller army units, namely 10 allotted cavalry regiments, one allotted cavalry squadron (Bohus) and one allotted cavalry company (Jämtland's), 22 allotted infantry regiments, eight enlisted cavalry units (organised before 1700) and 15 enlisted infantry regiments (also organised before 1700) and one enlisted artillery regiment. Within the allotment system there were in total 25,000 foot soldiers, 11,000 cavalry and also 6,600 sailors in the navy. If we summarise all enlisted units, Swedish and foreign, the total figure rose to 76,000 men.

But this considerable force was still not enough to meet the demands of a war against three enemies. During the first years of the war, 1700–07, before the start of the Russian campaign, another 14,700 men were raised in so-called three-, four- and five-*männing* regiments (see Appendix), five of cavalry and 12 infantry. These were a complement to the regular allotted regiments. Throughout the whole war another 6,400 men were organised in reduplication regiments (five cavalry and nine infantry). This meant that to the 36,000 regular soldiers within the allotment system another 21,100 were added within the system. No fewer than 31 new temporary units were organised within the allotment system, and so the whole system began to crumble, because it was not created for a long and costly war which demanded large numbers of replacements. The system was created for a defensive war against one enemy at a time, not the kind of war that the Great Northern War developed into. This would be more obvious the longer the war lasted.

In the Artillery Regiment in 1700 there were 1,488 men in the field artillery, of whom 623 were real artillery staff and a few hundred manning the artillery in the fortresses. At New Year 1714 the whole of the Artillery Regiment had a personnel of 1,308 men, 681 in the field artillery and 627 in the fortress artillery. The field artillery was, in 1714, based in the cities of Stockholm, Jönköping and Uddevalla, as well as the provinces of Scania and Jämtland, i.e. the different potential directions of operations, with Jönköping as a kind of operational reserve. The fortress artillery units were concentrated to eight larger fortresses, mainly in the west and south: Gothenburg, Bohus,

Marstrand, Halmstad, Malmö, Landskrona, Kristianstad, and Vaxholm in the Stockholm archipelago as well as a few smaller fortresses.

To this we can add 10,000 men in 10 so-called nobility dragoon battalions and 10 mining (mountain- or "bergs" battalions), 19 militia battalions and three rural militia regiments. Another 23,000 men were also enlisted for cash payment in Germany. Approximately 29 cavalry and 32 infantry units were enlisted for shorter or longer periods during the war.

In total this means that to the 76,000 regular soldiers (almost 70,000 in the army) we can add not less than 54,000 men in temporary units, allotted or enlisted, sometime during the war, to which we can add a few thousand men recruited among POWs, especially Saxons, but also French and Swiss soldiers. At its peak, at the beginning of the Russian campaign in the autumn 1707, the total Swedish army should have numbered about 115,000 men. Of them about 40,000 formed the army that Charles XII led into Russia.

Regulations

The relatively few regulations or instruction books that during the Carolean era were published for the infantry and cavalry could be described as rather simple drill instructions, rather far from any deeper literature in military theory. The only exception is a book written by lieutenant colonel Julius Richard de la Chapelles, *En militärisk exercitiebok eller regementsspegel av ett infanteriregemente* (*A military drill book or regimental mirror of an infantry regiment*) that was published in 1669. This is a classic in the history of Swedish military handbooks and regulations. Chapelles' book describes the specific tasks at all levels in the command structure in a regiment, from the ordinary soldier up to the colonel. These parts of the book can be described as an early version of leadership instruction. In the Carolean military world, as well as in the civilian one, everyone had his given role in the professional or social scene. Thus Chapelles offered everyone some guidelines:

The sergeant should organise the camp of the company every evening, when the regiment was on route march in the field, and he should also distribute the provisions among the men. The 1st class staff sergeant was responsible for the ammunition stores and should also inspect the men's muskets. The quartermaster should be updated on the situation in the company, which soldiers that were sick, commanded or missing of any other reason. He was also the one that could punish soldiers for smaller offences.

Above these was the ensign. He should be godly, with good morals and brave. He should also ask for pardon for poor soldiers that had made some minor offence. In this way the ensign would get the affection and respect of the men, of course with the ultimate purpose that the men in battle would fight extra hard to defend their ensign and the banner of the company. The lieutenant was closest to the company commander and should be skilful in drill. The captain himself should be like a father to his men, and especially ensure that lieutenants and other lower-ranking commanders did not bully the soldiers.

Above these company commanders there were the regimental commanders. The regimental quartermaster was responsible for arranging the camp of the whole regiment in the best way, while the major was responsible for the internal services such as guard posts and commanding men for different tasks.

He should also have knowledge of the exact strength of every company, and see to it that signals for reveille and parade were given at the right moment.

The lieutenant colonel should be the deputy of the regimental commander and could as such be somewhat milder towards the men than other officers, or as it is said by Chapelles: he should be "modest and familiar but somewhat serious". At the top of the hierarchy was of course the colonel, who should both love his King and have knowledge about every soldier. The colonel should also be skilled in the field, brave and decisive.

In the artillery several regulations were published during the late 17th and early 18th centuries, aimed at lower artillery staff, artillery engineers (fire workers) and sappers. A couple of these books were written by artillery colonel Johan Siöblad (1644–1710). In modern terms these were more educational instructions than regulations, but they were important parts of Sweden's first generation of military regulation books. All promotion within the artillery was supposed to through a degree pass, and it such a system these books were of great importance.

Within the artillery science an important contribution came from Daniel Grundell, an artillery captain at the Admiralty in Karlskrona, who in 1705 published *En kort inledning till artilleriet och Nödig underrättelse om artilleriet till lands och sjöss* (*A short introduction to the artillery and necessary information about the artillery at land and sea*). However, Grundell's book was partly based on outdated knowledge, although the writer said that it was based both upon practical experiments and his own experience.

The scientific revolution of the 17th century had provided a lot of new knowledge about how firepower and mobility of the artillery could be improved. But the difficulties in applying the discoveries of Galileo and Newton were initially considerable for many artillery officers. The Swede Niclas Rappe (1668–1727) complained in 1699 in his second book about the *Ernst-Fyrverkeriet* (*The serious firework*) on the difficulties to unite theory and practice: "But how many degrees You should direct the mortar and aim, there are many alternatives that several masters have strained their brains, but mostly in vain since the powder, weather, heat and cold cause that their theoretical calculations in practice show to be false." When you read these complaints it should be remembered that Rappe was one of Sweden's most experienced artillery officers. He had in 1689 served with the Imperial army that fought against the Turks in Hungary and was later a master fire worker in Dutch service.

Rappe and other writers wrote several educational books and regulations for fire workers, sappers and other professions within the artillery. But it was the versatile engineer Christoffer Polhem who became the first Swede to fully understand and develop the new scientific discoveries of ballistics. In 1717 Polhem published his book *Ett prov att visa bombers och kulors bågskott* (*A test to show the arc orbit of bomb and bullet shots*). His thoughts were later developed in another book in 1742. During the Great Northern War he was noticed for his invention of the rich screw that gave the Swedish field guns a much better accuracy.

After Poltava Lieutenant Colonel Rappe went into Russian captivity. During his years as a POW he wrote five books about different parts of the artillery science. Together with three that he had written already in

1699–1703, they formed *Överstelöjtnant Rappes Åtta Böcker Åhm Artilleriet* (*Lieutenant Colonel Rappe's eight books about the artillery*). It was all written by hand and finished in 1714, but could not be presented to Swedish readers until the writer returned home after the peace of Nystad in 1721.

The different parts described: I The construction of guns; II The Serious firework; III The entertaining firework; IV Geometry; V Reflexions about the artillery machines; VI Instruction of the establishing of artillery; VII The functions of the artillery staff, and VIII The defence of a breach. However, Rappe's book was to be printed, and only distributed in a few handwritten copies to a small number of executives. But his work marks an important step in the development of military science in Sweden, as the first attempt to take a holistic approach of the artillery, its structure, arms systems and tactical use in the field.

In 1720 the armoury master (*tygmästare*) Johan Möllerheim published *Artillerie (Artillery)*. He had already in 1706 published an important description of artillery equipment. Möllerheim was born in Bremen in 1674 and started his career in the Swedish artillery in 1688 at the age of 14, at Landskrona fortress. He came to live his whole life in the service of the artillery and died in 1721 or 1722.

Priests and Other Civilians

When the Carolean army was reformed in the 1680s and 1690s it was also in the era of the Lutheran orthodoxy. The religious knowledge of all Swedes was stipulated in a church law of 1686, and verified at regular house exams (*husförhör*) at the homes of both the nobility, burgers, farmers and other groups in Swedish society. The priests carried out the exams and noted the result of each and everyone in a specific book for every parish.

The religious control over officers and soldiers was, of course, also strict. Both Charles XI and Charles XII were of the opinion that all men in uniform should be Christian models. How that should be achieved was stipulated in the military legislation of 1683. Every morning and evening sermons should be held in the camp and everyone was obliged to be present when the trumpets and the drums called. When prayers were read, everyone should fall on his knees.

But the most important function of the priests was of course to encourage the men before the battle and prepare them for the possible risk of being killed. Models from the Bible were often used in sermons before battle, as well as a trust that they would wake for an eternal life at the Last Day. It was stressed that if the officer, NCO or soldier died, then it was according to God's will: "And if it now is Your will that I should fall, so provide me with a continuing belief in You, who is the right and living God."

The medical service in every regiment was maintained by one educated doctor, one surgeon and three assistants or journeymen. At their disposal they had a coffin with equipment. The army had also one pharmacist with responsibility for the field pharmacy, from which he handed out medicine to the different regiments. Every army staff with the highest ranking officers also had a doctor of its own, and of course also the King had his own doctor.

In order to work every regiment had a large number of craftsmen such as pistol smiths, saddlers and others, as well a variable number of civilian drivers and the servants.

4

Fortifications

Fortification troops became an independent type within the army in 1635. During Charles XI's reign they were divided into four brigades with the responsibility for fortresses in different parts of the country: the Stockholm brigade, the Gothenburg brigade, the Scanian brigade and the Finnish brigade. At the outbreak in 1700 the chief of fortifications, the general quartermaster, commanded 376 officers and men.

Immediately when the war broke out a special field fortification section was created with 25 officers and 12 craftsmen. Although that number seems very small, the unit's commander-in-chief, the general quartermaster in the field, had an important role being responsible for the army's marching order, quarters and reconnaissance. Many of the fortification officers also had the important task of supporting the operational planners with new-made maps.

In the year 1700 Sweden had a little more than 100 fortresses and fortlets, large and small, old and modern. The borders and coastlines were so extended that it was impossible to cover them all with modern, well-equipped and manned fortresses. Under Commander-in-Chief Erik Dahlberg (from 1696 general quartermaster) all fortresses were inventoried during the 1680s and 1690s, and decisions were made as to which were worth spending money on and which were better to be demolished, so that an invading enemy not would be able to use them as strongholds.

High priority was given to the 1680 founded naval base and city Karlskrona, as well as Gothenburg and Marstrand in the west as well as Kalmar in the east. In Scania in the south Malmö was modernised, and between 1667 and 1675 a new and modern fortress was built out of the older 16th century castle in Landskrona. Landskrona became the most modern of all Sweden's fortresses, built after the ideas of the French fortification engineer Sébastien Le Prestre de Vauban, although financial restrictions stopped some of the plans. Of the two other Scanian fortresses Kristianstad was in relatively good shape, but Helsingborg was precariously old. In Sweden's German provinces high priority was given to the work on Stralsund's fortifications in Pomerania, on Wismar in Mecklenburg further to the west and to Stade, close to the city of Bremen. At this time Stade was regarded as one of the most modern fortresses in northern Europe.

Erik Dahlberg warned repeatedly time after time in the years before the war that the fortresses in the Baltic provinces had to be restored in order to be able to halt a Russian invasion. But the money was not sufficient and most of it was spent on the most important places: Narva, Reval (Tallinn) and Riga together with Dünamünde (Daugavgriva) at the mouth of the river Düna (Daugava) in the Bay of Riga. The rest had to be more or less left to their destiny, regardless of their shape. The events in the first years of the war showed how much truth had been in Dahlberg's warning.

The most obvious deprioritization took place along Sweden's western border towards Danish-ruled Norway. A number of forts in the landscapes of Värmland, Dalarna and Jämtland were kept, but barely maintained and were given very weak garrisons, all as the result of hard priorities.

Fortification was (together with the artillery and the navy) the part of the armed forces where intellectual development had advanced most, with several published books about how to build, defend or besiege a fortress.

With Johannes Gezelius' 1672 book *Encyclopedia synoptica*, a broad presentation of modern knowledge in science, most aspects of fortification were described for the first time. Gezelius had been influenced by the Netherlands, and the same can be said about Lenaeus Wärnschiöld's *Fragmenter av fortifikationsfundamenterna* (*Fragments of the basics of fortification*) that was published in 1673. In these two books the reader is given an introduction to different concepts and definitions about fortresses, *Här ges läsaren en introduktion till olika begrepp och definitioner samt fästningarnas utförande och profil*. But the first deeper presentation of fortification in Swedish was a book written by the engineer captain Bart. Otto Smoll, *Architecturae militaris eller fortifikationskonstens korta undervisning* (*The military architecture or a short teaching in the art of fortification*) in 1693. Also in this book we meet influences from and praises of the Dutch art of fortification. According to Smoll knowledge of the Dutch fortification was essential since it was fundamental for all contemporary fortification at the end of the 17th century. But also Vauban's thoughts were presented by Smoll.

Vauban and the French school had their first introduction in Åke Rålamb's *Fortification eller Adlig övning* (*Fortification or noble exercise*). In this eighth volume of his instruction book for young noblemen that was published in 1691, Rålamb introduced both French and German writers in the field of fortification.

So, we find several important theoretical works about artillery and fortification in Sweden the years around 1700. But that does not mean that artillery or fortification were given priority in the warfare in the Swedish army. Swedish army tactics gave priority to high mobility and fast operations, an ideology that did not leave much space for protracted sieges. But there were exceptions, for instance the five-month-long siege of Torun 1703 and the siege of Grodno in 1706. With the exception of a few such examples the fortification warfare of the Swedish army was mostly about defending fortresses, not sieging them.

Already in the early years of the war the Russians penetrated deep into Ingria, Estonia and Livonia and several Swedish fortresses fell after shorter or longer sieges: Nöteborg (Sjlisselburg) 1702, Nyen (at the site of today's St Petersburg)

1703, Narva and Dorpat (Tartu) in 1704. But the greatest disaster came in 1710, after the defeat at Poltava. Now large Russian forces invaded the remaining Baltic provinces, and the large cities fell one by one: Riga with Dünamünde, Pernau, Reval and Viborg in south-eastern Finland. In a little more than a year after Poltava, fortresses with more than 10,000 men in their garrisons fell into Russian hands. Besides the strategic and operational disaster this meant that thousands of soldiers were lost at the same time as Sweden tried to raise another army to replace the one lost at Poltava.

3. Detail from a map showing Nyland's län (county) in Finland 1696, depicting fortification officers with their surveying instruments. Military Archives (Krigsarkivet)

The new strategic situation after the peace in 1721, with the loss of the Baltic provinces and south-eastern Finland meant a totally new situation for Swedish fortification planning, and a short glimpse of that reversed planning says a lot about the strategic consequences of the Great Northern War. A defence commission in 1723 said that the territorial losses during the war had allowed the Russian Tsar "to clear an open road almost into the heart of Svea Kingdom."

That was why already during the war the new strategic situations forced new thoughts about fortification, and in the autumn new sites for fortifications along what one surmised would be the new eastern border of Finland. Between 1723 and 1733 several studies were made concerning the defence of Finland as well as the eastern coastline of Sweden, since Russia once again was established along the Baltic Sea shoreline. The priorities were clear: the defence with the fortress of Fredrikshamn (this was before the construction of Sveaborg/Suomenlinna outside Helsinki began in the 1740s), Stockholm's archipelago with Fredriksborg and the passage at Vaxholm, and finally the inlet to Karlskrona.

The fortress of Jönköping was regarded as outdated and in a bad condition, and finally the castle burned down in 1737. Helsingborg's relatively modern fortress from the 1660s had been destroyed already in 1679, since it had not been of any help to stop a Danish invasion. Only the medieval tower Kärnan still stood, and it was kept since it functioned as a navigation mark. So the 14th century tower was saved for posterity.

Further to the south Malmö fortress was regarded as in good enough condition to be kept, with some reparations. But most important was Landskrona, with a harbour highly valued by the navy. For several decades before the start of the Sveaborg project, Landskrona was the fortress on which the highest amounts of money were invested. But Erik Dahlberg's plan to built 20 bastions around the city was never to be realised, for obvious financial reasons, neither during the Carolean era nor during the 18th century.

On Gotland, which in 1715 and 1717 hade been the goal for Russian landing raids, the defence problems were acute. The fortification efforts on the island were concentrated to the eastern coast where the fortress Karlsvärd was built outside the inlet to the harbour Slite. The construction of Enholmen had begun already in 1657, then came to a halt, then began again in 1711, since the Russians had taken Riga and Pernau just east of Gotland. But the work on Karlsvärd was not finished until 1771. This illustrates very well how many decades it took to build a fortification system that could compensate for the enormous territorial losses during the Great Northern War.

5

The Equipment and Tactics of the Army

Uniforms

The uniforms of the Swedish army developed step by step during the second half of the 17th century, in direction towards more standardised forms. In 1675, at the beginning of the war with Denmark in Scania, the principle was that every regiment should have a uniform in the colours of its province (red for Uppland, yellow for Södermanland etc.). This mix of colours within the army was replaced in 1687 with a blue coat, but with the facings in the colour of the province. That uniform model was inspired by the French army's coats, the *justacorps*.

This new uniform was used more or less unchanged into the 1690s. When older uniforms were worn out the soldiers were given the uniform of 1687. The exact look of the pockets, the number of buttons and other details could, however, differ between the regiments. The coats of this model had no collars, but from the mid 1690s collars began to be introduced on the uniforms.

The next step came during the winter 1706–07, which the army spent in Saxony. During this winter new regulations for the uniforms were issued. Among many new details the lower parts of the coats were made wider and the buttons ended at the waist. By that the "classic" Carolean uniform was created, the one that we meet on historic paintings. This new uniform was delivered to the regiments beginning in 1709–10, i.e. to regiments that had to be reorganised after Poltava. At the same time many regiments, especially enlisted ones, could still use the older model for several years.

The headgear was for a long time a cap with the flaps folded up, a so-called *karpus*. Different types of caps had been used by the Swedish army since at least the mid 17th century. Still, during the recess in Saxony the winter 1706 caps or rather hats with that look were used. But much is uncertain about the exact look of the different headgear. It seems that it was not until the new uniforms began to be frequently used after Poltava that the typical Carolean hat, the tricorne, was more generally used in the army. This is noteworthy because only the tricorne has become a symbol for the Carolean army, to the extent that it was introduced in the Swedish army as late as 1910, as an expression for the historical romanticism of that era.

4, 5. (top): Two of four *justacorps* supposedly brought from France to base the 'older' 1687 Swedish infantry coats on. It is however likely that at least three of the four coats are Prussian in origin. (Army Museum, Stockholm)

6. (right): *Justacorps* of Carl Wilhelm Drakenhielm, a lieutenant killed at the siege of Fredríkshald, the day before his king. The coat is described as having been a deep indigo with yellow lining and turnbacks with silver buttons. This coat seems to be a variant of the 1706 uniform, as it has no collar. (Army Museum, Stockholm)

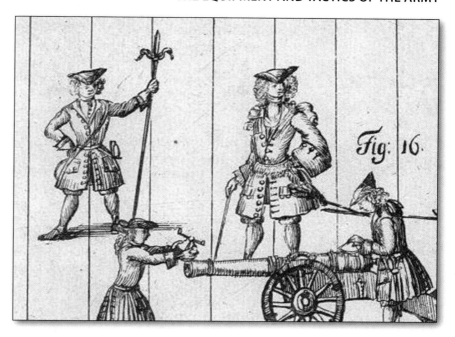

7. Contemporary image depicting artillery crew in fully formed tricornes. Army Museum, Stockholm.

All the time the basic rule was, of course, that older uniforms had to be worn out before the soldiers got the new models, which resulted in a mix between the units that was larger than copperplates and paintings give us reason to believe. Financial problems were growing, the longer war lasted. Particularly during the 1710s clothing became more and more simple, and very often the soldiers received new hats, stockings, gloves, coats or scarves at different times. Thus a regiment for instance could have coats of an older model and hats and scarves of a newer model. A total exchange of the whole uniform at the same time became more and more rare. The same continued through the 1720s, when many years could pass by before new garments were given, despite the fact that much had been worn out already during the last years of the war.

Arms and Armour

During the later part of the 17th century the matchlock musket and the long pike was the infantry armament in the Swedish army. It was only during the very last years of the century that flintlock muskets (often in the early version of the snaphance musket), often equipped with bayonets, became more and more common.

At the same time the shape of the musket was developed after inspiration from the internationally dominant "French type" with a thinner throat, that could be enclosed by the hand. During the years just before the turn of the century 1700 these two types of muskets lived side by side and the armament of the army was mixed. In 1688 new models of both matchlock and snaphance muskets were established. Both had a calibre just below 20 millimetres. In 1692 a model of infantry musket with flintlock and bayonet was established, and then followed by rather similar models in 1696 and 1699. During the war new infantry muskets were established in 1701, 1704 and 1716, but the differences were small between them and also compared with the models of the 1690s.

As usual it could take many years before a new model was delivered to the units and older and newer models came to exist side by side. Still, in the exercise regulations of 1701 it was presupposed that the soldiers were mostly equipped with matchlock muskets.

The specific command words for flintlock (snaphance) muskets with bayonet are used for the first time in 1708. But during the whole war also matchlock muskets were used in different militia units or among mustered peasants. Also, conquered Saxon muskets of both types were used to arm mustered peasants. At the taking of Thorn in 1703 about 9,000 Saxon muskets were taken in one enormous capture.

At the same time musket rests were removed step by step. In the 1670s about half of the soldiers still used rests to support their muskets, while the other half fought without that kind of support. But in a drill regulation issued in 1693 it is explicitly said that no musket rests should be used.

The muskets were manufactured in different factories around the country, with the most important one placed in Söderhamn in the southern part of Norrland. The whole production, from the raw material to the finished arms was controlled by the War College (Krigskollegium), the highest administrative body for the army.

Hand grenades were frequently used, and such a grenade was mostly a hollow ball made of iron, lead, earthenware with a diameter of 7–10 centimetres. They were filled with powder that was ignited from a burning fuse.

The carbines of the cavalry were, in a model from 1695, designed with a 75 centimetre long barrel, which made them 30 centimetrers shorter than the muskets of the infantry, of course in order to make them easier to handle on horseback. New models of carbine were designed in 1699 and 1704, but with only minor changes compared to the previous one.

Around 1700 the pistols were usually of a snaphance lock type. In 1694 a model of snaphance lock pistols was set and in 1695 another model for wheellocks, both for the cavalry. Charles XI had already decided in 1683 that the army's pistols should have a calibre of 16 millimetres, which became standard for Swedish army pistol all the way into the 19th century. But smaller abnormalities could occur: on the 1695 model the calibre was just below 16 millimetres. This meant that new pistol models in 1699, 1704, 1706 and 1716 did not deviate from the earlier ones. The probable difference was that the 1716 model was produced with both a short and a long barrel.

These models were often mixed with each other in the regiments, depending of what was in the armouries at the time. For instance, the Southern Scanian cavalry regiment in 1703 received 183 wheel lock carbines and 177 flintlock carbines. Three years later the same regiment received 1,000 new wheellock pistols.

The dragoons were equipped with an infantry musket and two cavalry pistols, which of course reflects that they should be able to fight both at foot and at horse.

The sword, or rather the small sword, is regarded as the most iconic weapon in the Carolean army, both for the contemporaries and in the

posterity, since is symbolises the offensive tactic of the army. Besides different kinds of officer's swords the simpler Carolean soldier's sword was the most important edged weapon. In the 1680s the Carolean sword had reached the fundamental construction it would keep for the following decades, and few changes were made. The blades were rounded, although there were some with punched blades, that is with a blood rim on the stronger side of the blade. The blood rim was, together with for instance ornaments on the plate, an obstacle for a smooth mass production. And mass production of swords was a priority for the Carolean army.

The sword had a stiff, two-edged blade made of three parts so it had a somewhat hexagonal cross section. The blade should be 89.1 centimetres long, but often it was 90–92 centimetres. At the end of the war the brass wire around the grip was replaced by leather, purely for financial reasons. So the sword was primarily made for stabbing, although it could be used for cutting to a limited extent.

Most of the Carolean swords were manufactured at Vira factory north of Stockholm. During the years 1701–18 no fewer than 217,000 swords of this model left that factory. Vira also produced 15,000 loose blades for the army.

A cavalry sword was designed in 1680 and came to be germinal for the cavalry sword in the coming years, although some minor changes were made. In 1704 the demand for a testing blow in the factory in order to check that the blade was hard enough was abolished. For the rest of the war it was sufficient that the blade could be bent in both directions. The demand for mass production during the war demanded a slight reduction of the very hard quality demands. This was the most important of a number of smaller adjustments that were made in order to make the mass production faster and cheaper, especially after Poltava.

Unlike the infantry sword, the cavalry sword usually, but not always, had a 17 centimetre-long blood rim on each side of the stronger part of the sword. It was also a little longer, almost 96 centimetres.

Officers' swords very often had a more individual touch, a remnant of the old tradition that the officer well into the 17th century was allowed to design his sword himself.

The pike, the long spear, was used during the last part of the 17th century by about one third of the infantry. The length was about the same as during the earlier decades of the century, usually around 4.7 metres (the head and ferule not included) and had a weight of a little more than three kilos. Drill instructions for pikes were issued in 1693 and 1701. Charles XII valued the pike highly because of what he regarded as its advantages during attacks, while several of his high ranking officers advocated a shift to muskets with bayonets, not least for their utility in both offensive and defensive battle. But it was after the King's death in 1718 that a general liquidation of the pikes first began. In November 1719 it was ordered that only one out of four infantry soldiers should be armed with pikes, and in the 1730s the process was completed and pikes were gone from the army. However, as late as the war against Russia in 1808–09 some militia soldiers were armed with old pikes taken out of the armouries, but that was more due to the lack of muskets and not a high valuation of the pikes.

The artillery had at the beginning of the war more than 3,700 guns at its disposal, or two guns for every soldier in the artillery. The explanation is, of course, that many guns were placed in fortresses with a very small garrison. The guns of the field artillery were only a minor part of the total number. Usually the field army of Charles XII hade at the most some 30 guns, mostly 3- and 6-pound regimental pieces or field guns, which could shoot projectiles of 1.5 or 3 kilos weight. The guns themselves had a weight of 200–400 and 900 kilos respectively. There were also a few 12-pound guns that fired 6 kilo projectiles and had a weight of some 1,300 kilos.

It is obvious that for an army tactic based on mobility and speed, heavy guns were not an advantage but an obstacle. At longer sieges heavier guns had a task to fulfil, but as we have seen, that was a relatively rare element in Carolean tactical behaviour.

The different fortresses of the empire were in 1699 armed with no fewer than 3,750 guns (of which 93 percent were cast of iron). In particular the Baltic fortresses had been reinforced with many new guns, although the fortification had not been modernised. Between 1673 and 1699 the number of guns in these fortresses had been tripled. The calibres varied, from the relatively small 3-, 4- and 6-pounders, to the heavier 8- and 12-pounders and the really heavy 18-, 24- and 36-pounders. While the guns shot projectiles along a flat track, there were also howitzers and mortars that shot projectiles in a higher and shorter track. The first howitzer was cast in Sweden as late as 1682. The usual howitzer calibre was 16-pound, but during the war 8-pounders were introduced, based upon experience during the campaigns in Lithuania and Poland in the early years of the war. There were mortars in a number of different calibres, from the small 3- and 6-pounder hand mortars, to 8-, 16-, 20-, 30-, 40-, 60-, 80-, 100, 150-, and 200- and all the way up to 300-pounders. The projectiles of the latter had a weight of about 150 kilos.

During the war a large number of fortresses fell into enemy, and especially Russian, hands and as a consequence the number of guns in the Swedish artillery was reduced. In 1720 the number had been reduced with about two thirds, down to about 1,100 guns.

Banners and Standards

A new system for the field signs of the army was introduced in 1672. Then the War College decided that the army should be provided with new banners and standards. The most important with them was that all provincial regiments (i.e. regiments recruited in a specific province or county) should have the coat of arms of that province on their banners. The life company of every regiment should have a white flag with the provincial coat of arms, while the other seven companies should have a flag in the colour of the province and the provincial coat of arms in the centre. This basic principle of using the provincial coat of arms is still used in the Swedish army for those regiments that have their origin in the old provincial regiments of the 17th century. In several provinces with a larger population more than one regiment was recruited, for instance in Småland and Västergötland, and in those cases the banners had to be designed differently.

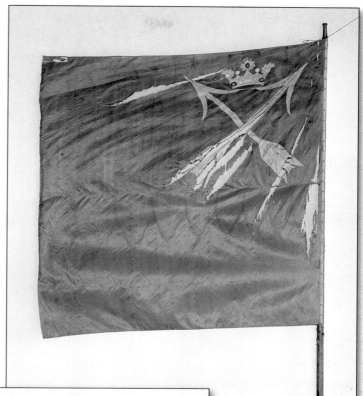

8. (right): Red taffeta company flag of Dalarna's three-männing regiment.

9. (below): Lieutenant colonel's flag, Östergötland standing company of Uppland's three-männing regiment.

Royal Armoury (Livrustkammaren), Stockholm

10. (left, top): Standard with Charles XII's name cipher in the centre.

11. (left, below): Flag, possibly from a dragoon regiment, bearing the cipher of Charles XII.

12. (below): Flag finial with monogram of Charles XII.

Royal Armoury (Livrustkammaren), Stockholm

In the cavalry regiments the life squadron had a white flag with the national coat of arms on one side and the King's name cipher on the other side. The other seven squadron standards had the provincial coat of arms on one side and the King's name cipher on the other. In the few dragoon regiments the banners of the life company was designed as in the life squadrons of the cavalry, while the other seven companies had the provincial coat of arms on both sides of the banner. The two highest ranked units, the Lifeguard of Foot and the Life Regiment of Horse, had white standards all through.

But the standardisation of the field signs was not easy to achieve, and in some cases there was no certain knowledge even about the exact provincial colours. This became obvious during the war with Denmark in 1675–79, as well as during the parallel war with Brandenburg. After an extensive investigation a new regulation about the army's banners and standards was issued in 1686. This new regulation was – for a short period in the mid 19th century – to be lasting, and is in important respects still current in the Swedish army.

The regulation of 1686 stipulated that in the allotted infantry regiments the life company should have a white flag with the national coat of arms on both sides, while the provincial coat of arms was placed in the upper, inner corner. The seven other company banners should have the colour of the province and the coat of arms of the same province in the centre, within a laurel. In the case that several regiments were recruited from the same province, different colour combinations were used.

For the cavalry standards the earlier system was more or less kept, so that the white flags of the life squadrons kept the national coat of arms on one side and the King's name cipher on the other side. For the other seven squadrons the provincial coat of arms and the King's name cipher on the respective sides was kept unchanged. The Life Regiment of Horse kept its white standards for all the squadrons.

These regulations were for the allotted regiments, while the system became less uniform for the enlisted regiments, without any clear provincial connection. For them the connection to the King himself was the fundamental. All life companies and life squadrons received white banners or standards, sometimes with the national coat of arms, sometimes other symbols. But for all other companies and squadrons the design could vary a lot. The only rule was that the design of the banners or standards were decided when the unit was organised.

If we should talk of some principle for the enlisted units, that would be the so called "Dutch manner", where the life banner or standard was white all the others within the regiment had a specific, but the same, colour, and all banners or standards of the regiment was given the King's crowned name cipher between two palm twigs. This design principle was used for the first time in 1688 when six infantry regiments were to be enlisted and sent to the Netherlands to participate in the Palatine succession war. This kind of design became very common during the whole Great Northern War, although modern research has reduced its dominance.

The size of the banners and standards was also decided in 1686. The infantry banners should be 180–190 centimetres in height and 210 centimetres in breadth. For the cavalry the standards, as always much smaller, should be

13. Two officers holding the banners of Tavastehus' infantry regiment in 1696; left: the white banner of the Life Company; right: the red banner of the other seven companies. Military Archives, Stockholm

square with every side 60 centimetres. Commonly, dragoon banners were also given sizes between the other two: 100 centimetres in high and 120 or 170 centimetres in breadth. Most commonly the banners or standards were made of damask cloth.

The only artillery regiment was split into numerous small field units and fortress garrisons, but they could not all be given banners. However in 1700 there was one artillery banner, transported on a special kettledrum wagon also with two kettledrums. As a consequence the lonesome banner was called the "kettledrum banner". The banner was white with the King's crowned name cipher, flanked by two standing and crowned lions. The design was completed with several minor symbols of artillery such as crossed guns, mortar, exploding grenades etc. Three royal crowns were also applied into each corner. The two kettledrums on the wagon were covered by with cloth with the same decor as the banner. The first known kettledrum banner for the artillery is from 1700, and the next one from 1716.

The fundamental rule was that the infantry banners should have their decor painted, while for cavalry standards embroidered edging should be used. The latter was much more expensive, but also more hardwearing. However, the system was flexible and we have examples not only of painted infantry banners, but also those where embroidering edging, intarsia or appliqué has been used.

Many banners and standards were for obvious reasons destroyed during the war, while others today are preserved in a more or less worn out condition, especially in Danish and Russian trophy collections. But the foremost banner painter of the Carolean period, Olof Hoffman, made in the years 1687–88 painted copies on paper of all the army's banners and standards, a work that is still kept at the Military archives (Krigsarkivet) in Stockholm. Thanks to Olof Hoffman we still have a more or less complete picture of the banners and standards of the army, and how they were designed just a few years before the outbreak of the Great Northern War. Some preserved original banners show that there were minor discrepancies between the paper drawings and the original flags, but that does not change the overall picture.

More importantly there was no immediate exchange of banners and standards after the 1686 regulations were issued. As always the old ones were used as long as possible, until they were worn out. This is especially the case with embroidered standards. Several cavalry regiments used during the whole 1700–21 war, standards that they had been given during the 1670s. When the North Scanian cavalry regiment surrendered at Poltava in 1709 they laid down standards that the regiment had been given in 1665, after 44 years of use.

The banners and standards for the contemporary regiments organised during the war became more uniform, since these units did not have any older traditions or flags to take into account. Already from the year 1700 and onwards new reserve units for the allotted regiments, the so-called männing regiments, as well as reduplication regiments and estate dragoons were organised. For them it was decided that any new organised unit should have banners or standards in the same colour as the regular provincial regiment, but also here with the exception for the white life companies. In the inner, upper corner of every banner or standard the provincial coat of arms should be painted. Units recruited from several provinces, as well as the mining units and the estate dragoons, all received blue flags.

These rules seem to have been followed for the very first years, but when new männing regiments were organised in 1703 more divergences from the rules of 1700 occurred, sometimes with the approval of higher authorities, sometimes as a result of the initiative of the regimental commander. The life banners or standards more and more often also had the name cipher of the King. Sometimes older banners were used, probably for financial reasons. An extreme example was Nyland and Tavastehus counties' reduplication cavalry regiment that was equipped with standards from the days of the Thirty Years' War!

The rules of 1686 were often used as a guideline when units were organised in the provinces of Ingria, Estonia and Livonia or in Sweden's German provinces. But here we also have a much larger variation than for the units in Sweden proper.

After the Poltava disaster in 1709 many regular units were organised again and new banners and standards were produced for the new allotted regiments. Most of them, also for the cavalry, were painted, for obvious financial reasons. Even more financial restrictions can be traced in the following years. In 1712–13 several new männing regiments were raised and after the surrender of a Swedish army at Tönningen in 1713 it was once again time to raise the regular allotted regiments. Now there were no possibilities the follow the regulations of 1686. If possible older banners and standards still kept in the stores were could be used they were handed out to the units, otherwise every effort was made to produce as cheap new ones as possible. During the last years of the war some local arrays or bands organised by farmers were organised, and they were given very simple county banners (*häradsfanor*) or array or band banners (*uppbådsfanor*), mostly with the name cipher of the King, the year the unit was raised and sometimes the name of the county on a single coloured flag.

However, from 1715 the observance of the regulations of 1686 and 1700 was more rigorous, which of course had to do with Charles XII's return to Sweden from his Turkish exile. Already by 1716 the Lifeguard of Foot had received new, painted, banners, while the Life Dragoon Regiment in 1718 received new standards made with embroidered edging. The next regiment in turn was the Life Regiment of Horse, but the new standards were not distributed before Charles XII was killed in November 1718. After that the royal name cipher had to be changed, and when the regiment finally received their new standards they bore the name cipher of the King crowned in 1720, Fredrik I.

Battle Tactics

It has for many years been regarded as a "truth" that the Carolean army was more offensive than its enemies, in fact than most of the contemporary armies. Even in difficult situations priority was given to the offensive rather than the defensive. But modern research has modified that picture. The Swedish army under Charles XII certainly used offensive tactics, but in the fundamentals that hardly differed so much from that of Danish, Saxon or Russian adversaries. But the distinguishing quality of the Swedish army, especially before Poltava, was its good training and discipline. With very well trained soldiers the Swedes were able to conduct offensive tactical moves even in difficult situations, when maybe another army would have chosen a more defensive tactic. The Carolean soldiers had been very well trained in drill, but it was not movements for parade, it was turns and other movements in battle that were drilled into them.

It is here that we find the special nature of Swedish battle tactics, namely the *prerequisites* for advanced and sometimes very hazardous offensive tactics, more than deviant tactics in themselves.

Of course the ideal of the tactical instruction books is not the same as the reality of the battlefield. The particular nature of a specific combat situation, the number of casualties, losses of weaponry, the degree of lesser-trained and experienced recruits, all of those affect tactical behaviour. But still it is clear that the Carolean army's tactical behaviour very often was close to the ideal of the instruction books, also many years after the original army had been lost at Poltava.

The combination of fire and, above all, movement was decisive, while these factors also worked for the protection of the soldiers, thus forming the classical military trinity. Not least the importance of taking and holding the initiative, especially if the Swedes were inferior in number, resulted in very offensive tactical behaviour.

The Swedish infantry regiment was composed of eight companies of 150 men each, and of two battalions of 600 men each. The company was the smallest tactical unit, but also the battalion formation was very often used as a tactical unit. Two thirds of the men were armed with muskets and one third with pikes. During marches the men were divided into six divisions, four of musket and two of pike. The latter marched in the middle of the column, so that the regiment could swiftly regroup to a combat formation. In every company there were also 12 grenadiers, with the task of throwing hand grenades.

The bayonet had made its entrance into the Swedish army during the 1690s, but the pike was still the most important shock weapon of the infantry. The musketeers were also equipped with swords.

In combat formation the pikemen were placed in the middle, while the musketeers stood on both wings. They only shot one fusillade, usually at as short a distance as possible, some 70 paces from the enemy. Immediately after that the whole company (or battalion) charged into the enemy lines with lowered pikes or bayonets and drawn swords. For grenadiers it was essential that they also fired their muskets at the same time as the other musketeers. Immediately after that every grenadier should hang his musket on his back, grab, light and throw a grenade, before with lowered bayonet he followed his comrades in the charge.

In order to keep the company together the banner, worn by the ensign, had a crucial importance as a signal instrument and mark of gathering. If the banner was lost to the enemy, the possibility for the company to fight a well organised combat was severely reduced.

There is an important word in this context: the word *trust*. The company, at least in the allotted regiments, consisted of officers, NCOs and soldiers who lived in the same region, went to church together and often lived next door to each other. They had had drills together outside the church, at the captain's residence or on the exercise field of the regiment, which of course created a feeling of fellowship. Such factors were of greater importance in the allotted than in the enlisted regiments, and were of course weaker especially in those regiments that had been recruited very hastily without taking any drills together before they were sent to the field army.

But maybe even more important for the creation of trust between the soldiers, was that the soldiers cooked for themselves. Every company was joined by three provisioning carriages, except for carriages with breadbaskets and water sacks. These wagons transported the two steel mills of the company, and then the flour was handed out to the soldiers. Six soldiers formed a tent team who not only shared the same tent, but had a common fireplace outside the tent, where they cooked their food or baked their bread. The importance of the tent teams can hardly be overestimated, because here was the hard, inner core that was so extremely important in order to keep the companies together, and by extensions larger units, especially when they were under severe pressure, not least in combat. It was obvious that the Carolean army understood the importance of trust and how to build that up starting with the little group, the tent team.

In an army that preferred a tactical offensive the cavalry of course played a very important role. The 8,000 allotted cavalrymen in the year 1700 all had about the same background as their fellow infantrymen, and exactly like them the cavalry men were drilled in movements and fighting and battle tactics long before the outbreak of the war. The cavalry was the hard-hitting club of the Carolean army, with the mission to break up enemy formations and lines. This is very clear if we bear in mind that the Swedish army had relatively few and small dragoon units, and almost all mounted units were traditional cavalry.

Here we find one of the most important differences between the Swedes and the Russian army. Russia had a large number of dragoon units in order to be able quick move forward troops that could fight as infantry, while the Russians at the same time were weaker that the Swedes in mounted combat.

The horses in the Swedish cavalry differed from those in the enemy armies. Most of the horses were Swedish, for the very simple reason that it was expensive to import them. The usual Carolean combat horse, *klipparen* ("the clipper"), was smaller than Continental horses. It should measure at least 1.4 metres in height behind the saddle, but it is clear that even shorter horses were approved if they could meet the other demands for strength etc. These Swedish horses were strong with good fitness, despite the fact that many of them were hardly larger than a modern pony. The horse should also manage to carry a soldier of say 70 kilos, saddle equipment of 16 kilos, arms and equipment of 25 kilos and provisions and packing of another 24 kilos, in total at least 135 kilos.

A lot of attention was also given to breeding. Stallions and mares were imported from France, Norway and also from Swedish Livonia and Pomerania. These horses were sent to royal stud farms that provided the Lifeguard Corps (*Livdrabantkåren*) and the Life Regiment of Horse. In the rest of the army every company or squadron had to take care of its own horses, with up to 15 mares and some stallions for every squadron.

The cavalry regiments used valacks, often with powerful legs and thick chests. Usually these horses served for between four and 10 years, but there were examples of horses that stayed in the army for up to 20 years.

During the campaign in Saxony in the autumn of 1704 there were examples of Swedish cavalry units that, partly in combat, moved 300 kilometres in only five days and nights, which gives us an idea of the capacity of their horses.

The foreign enlisted regiments in Swedish service, especially German, most commonly had horses that did not differ from those in other Continental cavalry units.

Besides riding horses, of course numerous baggage horses were used, sometimes mobilised among the local population, in Sweden or abroad. An ordinary complete cavalry regiment had 204 riding horses for the officers and 1,000 for the privates, but also 435 baggage horses. Of course there were also numerous riding and baggage horses both in infantry regiments as well as in the artillery. The Swedish army that in 1707 broke up for the march into Russia counted 43,600 men and 35,000 horses.

Swedish cavalry tactics were inspired by Louis XIV's France, but had been perfected even further as an assault weapon. The fundamental aim was, as it is said in one of the regulations, "to as soon as possible look the enemy in the whites of his eyes". Charles XI personally engaged himself in the development of cavalry tactics and the drill of the mounted units. Their skill was controlled during numerous manoeuvres led by the King in the 1680s and 1690s. It was then, as was the case in many other aspects, tactics were developed and trained, that were later used during the campaigns of Charles XII. Also the horses were drilled by the firing of loose shots, fires were ignited with strong smoke, drums were beaten and trumpets were blown, all to make the horses accustomed to the noise of the battlefield or the field in general.

The basic battle formation for the cavalry squadron or company (both words were used) was that the 125 men formed themselves three lines. In the centre of the first line was the ensign (or cornet) riding with the standard, the checkpoint of the squadron. The men should ride so tight that every man in the right wing should hold their left knees behind the right knee of the comrade next to their left side. Correspondingly the men in the left wing should hold their right knees behind the left knee of the comrade next to their right side. Thus the squadron formed a snowplough formation when they rode to attack.

Every cavalryman was armed with a sword, a carbine and two pistols. The basic tactic was an attack "*i fullt rännande*" ("in full gallop") with drawn swords to stab with. Very often the cavalry charge was made without any preparation, by firing pistols.

The artillery had during the time of Gustavus Adolphus during the 1620s and 1630s developed into a mobile and integrated arm, and thus been able to increase the fire power of the army without reducing its mobility. That tradition was not totally forgotten during the Carolean era, but now the strong emphasis on a fast and powerful attack had reduced the importance of the field artillery. Guns were used for preparatory fire and sometimes (as was the case at Poltava) they were simply left behind when the attack started. As we will see later it was not until the battle at Gadebusch in 1712 that the artillery, thanks to several technical inventions, once again came to play a decisive role in the tactic of the Swedish army.

Amphibious tactics were of course of great importance for an army that operated in the Baltic Sea region, where many operations were a combination of a land and sea battle. Islands or groups of islands such as the Danish islands, Gotland, Öland, Åland and Ösel (Saaremaa) all demanded some kind of amphibious warfare, offensive or defensive. The same can be said for the coastlines and the narrow straits, as between the Danish islands, at Öresund, along the northern German coast, in the Swedish and Finnish archipelagos, along the Gulf of Bothnia, the Gulf of Finland and the Bay of Riga, as well as along many of the larger Swedish and Finnish lakes, Ladoga and Peipus on the border between Sweden and Russia. In all these operational areas some kind of amphibious capability was required.

This was clearly demonstrated directly after the outbreak of the war in 1700, when Denmark was forced to leave the war through a Swedish landing on Zealand. After the Danish attack on Sweden's allied Holstein-Gottorp the Swedish navy went to sea in the summer of 1700: 38 ships of the line and eight frigates with in total 2,700 guns and 15,000 crew. Together with 13 Dutch and 12 English ships the Danes were very inferior and could not prevent a Swedish landing on the shores of Zealand, north of Copenhagen. Before dawn on 25 July 1700 almost 5,000 Swedish soldiers boarded 66 different landing craft that took them the last 600 metres to land, while the guns of the allied fleet bombarded the Danish positions. After two hours of fighting a Swedish bridgehead was established, and a second wave landed and then almost 10,000 Swedish soldiers were ready to attack towards Copenhagen further south along the coastline.

In that situation King Frederik IV of Denmark decided to give up before the disaster was completed. On 8 August a peace treaty was signed between

Denmark and Sweden's allied Holstein-Gottorp, and the Swedish invasion force could embark on the ships again.

A very different type of amphibious operation took place with the crossing of the river Düna (Daugava) at Riga in 1701. Having spent the winter of 1700–01 in a camp in north-eastern Estonia, Charles XII led his army towards Swedish Riga, in order to break a Saxon siege of the city.

South of the river some 20,000 Saxon and some Russian soldiers were positioned, while the King advanced with 7,000 Swedes. But instead of reinforcing Riga's garrison Charles chose to attack across the river, towards an army three times larger than his own. Flat-bottomed boats were built and constructed with high screens for protection against enemy fire. Also four blockhouses, each with 10 guns, were launched into the river. Several Swedish naval ships had also sailed along the river up to Riga. In total that gave the Swedish attacking force a considerable firepower. Wet straw was also set on fire in order to create a smokescreen in front of the Swedish forces.

The landing occurred at a point were the Saxon army was relatively weak, and thus a bridgehead not only was taken, it also managed to resist Saxon counterattacks. Protected by the own artillery on the river and the conquered position on the southern shore, the Swedes began to construct a floating bridge over to the bridgehead, but hard winds made it impossible to finish it. Instead, reinforcements of men and horses had to be transported over Düna by boat, which gave the Saxon army time to retreat in good order before the Swedes were ready to pursue them.

The Swedish army managed to make an amphibious operation across the river Düna against a combat-ready and superior enemy, and also relieved Riga from the siege. It was a great tactical victory, but the operational and strategic victory failed since the Saxon army and their Russian allies managed to escape in relatively good order.

6

The First Phase of the War, 1700–1709

The expansion of the Swedish empire had also resulted in a number of revanchist neighbours along the new borders in the east, south and west.

The Danish hereditary enemy not only wanted to reconquer the former Danish and Norwegian provinces that had been lost to Sweden in the peace treaties of 1645 and 1658. Denmark also feared, not without a reason, to be surrounded by Sweden and her close allies south of Denmark, Holstein-Gottorp. In the commonwealth of Poland-Lithuania, also in a personal union with Saxony, there was a deep wish to take back lost influence in Livonia and the city of Riga, taken by the Swedes in 1621. Finally Russia, had never given up its ambition to once again get back to the shores of the Baltic Sea. That ambition had been there since the large Russian territorial losses to Sweden in peace treaties in 1595 and especially 1617.

The three powers formed an alliance in 1699, but did not manage to coordinate their efforts, so declared war against Sweden at different times in 1700. This gave Sweden an opportunity to strike against one of them at a time. In the summer of 1700 a Swedish amphibious landing on Zealand, supported by naval units from England and the Netherlands, managed to push Denmark out of the war. After that the Swedish army was transferred to Estonia where in November 1700 it broke up a Russian siege of the Swedish garrison in the city of Narva, and at the same time inflicted on the Russian army a crushing defeat.

Having spent the winter in a camp in Lais in north-eastern Estonia, the Swedish army advance towards the south-west, were a Saxon-Polish army, with some allied Russian troops had for several months besieged Riga. After a swift surprise amphibious operation the Swedes managed to cross the river Düna and drive away the Saxon army and its allies.

Now the immediate threats towards Sweden had been removed, the question was, what now? Denmark had left the war, so Charles XII and his advisors had to choose between attempts to give either the Poles or the Russians the final blow. Charles XII chose to start with August the strong of Saxony-Poland, obviously with a hope that a victory here would give him Polish allied troops for the final campaign against the Russians.

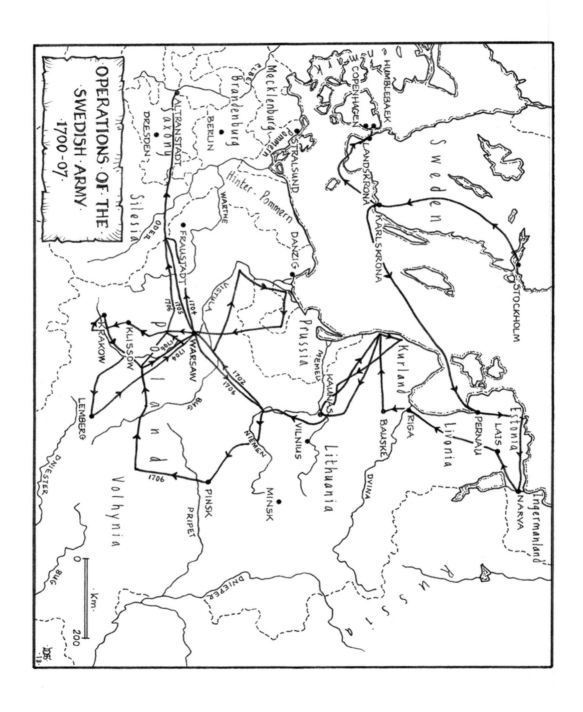

OPERATIONS · OF · THE ·
SWEDISH · ARMY ·
1700 - 07 ·

This choice has been discussed for almost 300 years. The attack with the main Swedish army against the south, through Courland and Lithuania into Poland left the eastern border more or less open for Russian infiltration into Sweden's Baltic provinces. Not the least, modern historians have criticised Charles XII, suggesting a stronger defence against the east would have prevented the Russian penetration of Ingria, Estonia and Latvia that step by step resulted in a Swedish lost of control of the area. But new research has stressed that the Baltic provinces, and especially Estonia, had suffered severely during the great famine in 1696–97, when about one third of the population died. After that there was no possibility that a large Swedish field army could be provided for a longer time, so the Swedes had to go towards the south in order to avoid starvation. Theoretically the only alternative was an offensive deep into north-western Russia, towards Pskov and Novgorod and then further into central Russia and Moscow. But it is far from certain that these areas could feed a large army.

This whole discussion shows one thing: it was now in 1701–02 that several decisive strategic decisions were made, that came to have a profound effect on the war for several years.

At the beginning of the campaign the Swedes conquered large areas of Poland, including the cities of Klissow (Kliszów), Danzig (Gdansk), Thorn (Tórun) and Lemberg (Lviv). The Polish army led a large defeat at Klissow in July 1702, and in 1704 Stanisław Leszczynski became King of Poland after the deposed Polish-Saxon ruler August II ("August the Strong"). This was an election that was made after very strong Swedish pressures, and the new King of Poland also closed a peace with Sweden in November 1705.

But Leszczynski never managed to get control over any larger parts of Poland, and Polish forces loyal to August continued the war, together with the Saxon army. However a new defeat against the Swedes at Fraustadt in February 1706 did not stop the war, so Charles XII invaded August's German land, Saxony, and then managed to press him to sign a peace treaty in Altranstädt in September 1706.

However, during these years of Swedish campaigning in Poland and also Saxony, Russia had managed to rebuild her army after the disaster at Narva. Tsar Peter I ("the Great") pushed for a modernisation of the Russian army, and the young Russian navy (founded as late as in 1696, mainly after the pattern of Western Europe, and not the least Sweden). Although a Russian army had been beaten by the Swedes in a battle at Gemäuerthof in Courland in July 1705, the Russian military threat against Sweden kept rising, deeper and deeper into the countryside of Ingria, Estonia and Livonia. In 1702 Nöteborg (Schlijsselburg) fell into Russian hands, in 1703 Nyen (which was demolished and the new city of St Petersburg began to be built in May 1703, on the ruins of the Swedish town. In 1704 Dorpat fell into Russian hands.

But instead of sending larger forces to rescue these provinces Tsar Peter decided to strike directly towards Russia's heart. In August 1707 more than 40,000 Swedish soldiers left Saxony for the long march towards the east.

It began as a very successful march. At Grodno in eastern Poland in January 1708 the Russian army led another crushing defeat, and in July the same year a Russian force was defeated at Holovzin (Holowczyn). This was to be the last great victory of the Carolean army against their Russian enemy.

The Swedish army advanced deeper and deeper into Russia directly towards Moscow. To conquer Moscow was not a goal in itself, but it was a way to attract Peter and the main Russian army to risk a decisive battle, a battle that Charles XII was convinced he would win. With such a victory the Russian gains in Sweden's Baltic provinces would easily be rolled back.

However the Russians refused to risk this decisive battle and retreated, while disturbing the Swedes with minor attacks and destroying their opportunities to feed men and horses. So, in September 1708 a Swedish rescue army advanced from Riga with a large convoy of baggage carriages with the supplies so much needed in the main army. But at a battle of Lesnaja in eastern Poland (today in Belorussia) the Swedish army was defeated by the Russians. Several thousand Swedish soldiers managed to escape and reach the main army, but all the supplies were lost.

Now Charles XII had no choice. A further advance to the east and Moscow would result in starvation, and a retreat to the west back into Poland would mean that the whole attempt of forcing Tsar Peter to a decisive battle had to be given up. So, Charles chose a third alternative, to take the army to the south and Ukraine where it could survive the coming winter and then make a new attempt to crush the Russian main army the next spring and summer. In the Ukraine the Swedes also found an ally in the anti-Russian Cossacks under their hetman Mazepa.

But instead Tsar Peter followed the Swedes into the Ukraine and an overwhelming Russian force crushed the Swedish army at Poltava on 28 June 1709. Three days later the main part of the Swedish army surrendered to the Russian at Perevolotjna. In total over 20 000 prisoners were taken – Swedes, Germans, Estonians, Livonians and some Poles – and formed large columns that under the burning summer sun of the Ukraine had to march up to Moscow for Peter's grand victory parade. After that they were sent to numerous prisoner-of-war colonies in European Russia as well as in Siberia.

At the last minute Charles XII managed to escape with some 1,000 men into the Turkish province of Moldavia. Immediately the news of what had happened at Poltava spread over Europe and new declarations of war arrived from both Denmark and Saxony, both throwing themselves over what they hoped was the mortally wounded Swedish lion.

7

The Second Phase of the War, 1710–1721

The Developing Disaster, 1710–15

In November 1709 Danish forces landed on the beaches at the small fishing villa Råå, just south of Helsingborg in north western Scania. They advanced into Scania from their bridgehead, but already on 28 February 1710 a Swedish army under the command of Magnus Stenbock managed to beat the invading Danish army at Helsingborg. The remaining of the Danish forces had top retreat back to Zealand, and so ended their last effort to reconquer Scania.

When the Russian general Sjeremetjev launched his summer offensive in 1710 the last Swedish positions in the eastern provinces began to fall: Pernau in Estonia, Viborg in south-eastern Finland and Dünamünde just west of Riga in Livonia. In July Riga's garrison gave up the struggle against hunger, plague and a Russian bombardment. On 30 September 1710 Reval also gave up, the last Swedish city in the Baltic provinces. In December the last Swedish soldiers were evacuated from the island Ösel, and an attempt to reconquer Ösel in 1711 failed.

After his great successes in the north-west Tsar Peter had to move his attention towards the south and the Ottoman Empire. All the time since his escape after Poltava in 1709 King Charles XII had tried to convince the Sultan Ahmed III to join the war. The Sultan and his advisors were reluctant, but in July 1711 a Turkish army advanced and managed to surround the Russian main army, including Peter himself, at Prut. But against all odds Peter managed to resolve the situation with negotiations, he and his army escaped from the trap and the Turkish army was withdrawn. This was a disaster for Charles XII.

During the year 1712 Denmark had launched an offensive in northern Germany and conquered the Swedish fortress of Stade in Bremen-Verden, while allied Saxon and Russian forces intensified a siege of Stralsund, a siege initiated in 1711. To save its German provinces, Sweden sent an army of 10,000 men under Magnus Stenbock, the man who just had saved Scania from the Danes. He managed to defeat the Danish army at Gadebusch in December 1712; the last Swedish victory of the war.

OPERATIONS OF THE
SWEDISH ARMY
·1707-18·

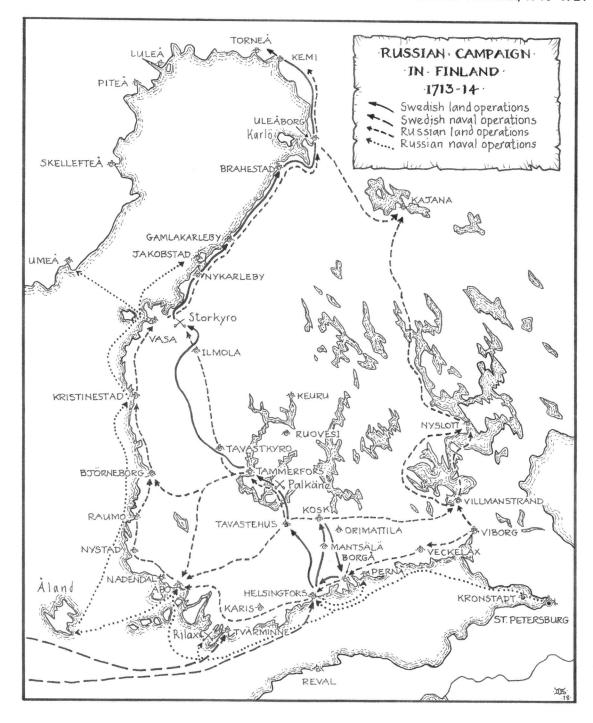

RUSSIAN · CAMPAIGN ·
· IN · FINLAND ·
· 1713-14 ·

Swedish land operations
Swedish naval operations
Russian land operations
Russian naval operations

TORNEÅ
KEMI
LULEÅ
PITEÅ
ULEÅBORG
Karlö
SKELLEFTEÅ
BRAHESTAD
KAJANA
GAMLAKARLEBY
JAKOBSTAD
UMEÅ
NYKARLEBY
Storkyro
VASA
ILMOLA
KRISTINESTAD
KEURU
RUOVESI
NYSLOTT
TAVASTKYRO
BJÖRNEBORG
TAMMERFORS
Palkäne
RAUMO
KOSKI
VILLMANSTRAND
TAVASTEHUS
ORIMATTILA
NYSTAD
MANTSÄLÄ
VIBORG
BORGÅ
VECKELAX
Åland
NADENDAL
PERNA
ÅBO
HELSINGFORS
KRONSTADT
KARIS
ST. PETERSBURG
Rilax
TVÄRMINNE
REVAL

14. Magnus Stenbock. By Georg Engelhard Schröder. Stenbock served with the army of the United Provinces and saw action along the Rhine and at Fleurus in 1690. He saw service with the Swedish army at Narva, Dünamünde, Klissow, Cracow and at Pułtusk. He led Swedish troops to victory at Helsingborg and Gadebusch. National Museum, Sweden

But there were no opportunities for Stenbock to advance towards the south, in order to reach the Ottoman empire where Charles XII wanted a Swedish army so he could persuade the Turks into a united Swedish–Turkish war against Russia. As long as no Swedish army arrived, there was no hope for a new Turkish campaign against Russia. But Stenbok's army never came to Turkey, instead it was forced to surrender to the Danes and allied Saxon and Russian forces in the fortress of Tönningen, at the western coast of Holstein, in May 1713. Soon thereafter Sweden's ally Holstein-Gottorp was occupied by Danish forces.

Already in 1710 Great Britain and the Netherlands, supported by the emperor in Vienna, suggested that Sweden's Pomerania should be neutralised, kept by Sweden but not used as a base for Swedish military operations. The government in Stockholm accepted the idea, but King Charles XII refused. Then Pomerania could no longer be saved. Besides the Danish, Saxon and Russian attacks in 1712–13, Preussen and Hannover joined the coalition since both had territorial ambitions in the area. On 12 December 1715 Stralsund fell after a long siege and in April 1716 Wismar surrendered, the last stronghold in Sweden's German provinces.

By an even more dangerous situation had developed for Sweden in the east. In the summer of 1712 General Admiral Fjodor Apraksin led a Russian army across the River Kymmene in south-eastern Finland, but the defenders under General Lybecker managed to drive the enemy back. However the following year, 1713, a larger Russian force (about 16,000 men) launched another attack, and now advanced fast into southern Finland. At the same time a Russian fleet of shallow rowing galleys operated in the Finnish archipelago, in close coperation with the Russian main army, and attacked behind the Swedish defensive positions. In August 1713 Finland's largest city, Åbo (Turku) fell into Russian hands and in February 1714 a Swedish army was defeated at the battle of Storkyro in north-western Finland. Finland had fallen into Russian hands, and a wave of more than 20,000 civilian refugees welled over to the western part of the realm, while Russian forces occupation the Åland islands and also attacked and burned the city of Umeå on the Gulf of Bothnia.

Such was the situation when in the autumn 1714 Charles XII left Turkey and after an intensive ride through eastern Europe managed to reach the besieged Stralsund, which he left before the city's surrender. On 13 December 1715 he landed with a few companions at the shore of Scania, not far for Trelleborg, 15 years after he had left Sweden proper for the battle at Narva.

Now intensive activity began to raise new troops and put the whole country, or rather what was left of it, on a war-footing. At the same time diplomatic channels were used to ease the desperate situation. London, and especially the leader of Britain's foreign policy Lord Bolingbroke, said that it was now time to save King Charles XII against his own will, and that was rather a good description of the situation.

In 1713 the council or government in Stockholm had already urged the King to accept a British offer for mediation, in order to achieve the peace that "Your Majesty's faithful subjects loudly" ask for. But the King still had strong support among the three lower estates (the clergy, burghers and farmers) in the parliament (riksdagen). Charles XII used that situation in a major attempt to redirect the whole nation for a total war effort.

Sweden and Total War, 1716–18

The term "total war" is of course a 20th century phenomena, but it can very well be used to describe what happened in Sweden the years 1716–18.

When Charles XII returned to Sweden in December 1715 he chose the city of Lund for his headquarters, and with that bypassed the Council and the bureaucracy in Stockholm. Instead he chose the diplomat and financier Georg Heinrich von Görtz from Holstein as his special troubleshooter. Görtz soon became the most influential individual in both foreign and financial policy besides the King himself.

Although the military situation was extremely dark, there were some diplomatic possibilities. King August in Saxony-Poland saw how Livonian territories that he regarded as Polish now had been conquered by the Russians, and Prussia, Hannover and Great Britain were highly suspicious when Russian forces advanced as far westwards as Mecklenburg. In Copenhagen a planned Russian invasion of Scania supported by the Danish navy in 1716 was cancelled because of Denmark's suspicion of the Russian intentions, and 20,000 Russian soldiers that had already been concentrated on Zealand had to go home. Görtz tried to use these frictions among the enemies, and especially to play out Great Britain against Russia. But at the same time in May 1718 he started direct peace negotiations on Åland with a Russian delegation led by Andrej Osterman.

While Görtz was playing the diplomatic card a new Swedish army was organised and extra taxes were taken out, including a new wealth tax based upon a tax return, a totally new phenomenon in Sweden. In order to bypass both the council and the parliament a so-called purchase deputation (Upphandlingsdeputationen) was created. Formally it was led by the Holstein general von Dernath, but in reality the deputation was governed supreme by Görtz. In 1716–18 Görtz governed what in really was an armament ministry.

In order to finance the military mobilisation, different forms of state bonds were produced, also in smaller denominations. That way Görtz got control over large parts of the state income. His deputation also issued so-called emergency coins, and at the time of Charles XII's death in November 1718 more than 25 million emergency coins were circulating on the Swedish market. The state also forced churches and hospitals to change their cash to state bonds. All these measures could of course only result in a fast-growing erosion of the general trust in the payment means. The hope by Charles XII,

15. Clockwise from left: uniform worn by Charles XII when killed at Fredrikstad, 30 November 1718; wig said to have been worn by him during the 1714 campaign; close-up of the boots and gloves worn by him at Fredrikstad, 1718. Royal Armoury (Livrustkammaren), Stockholm.

Görtz and their advisors was of course that the war situation would improve before a financial collapse took place.

The Navy as the Last Line of Defence

During the 1710s the Russian navy expanded very fast, and could now also use the harbours of Riga, Pernau, Reval and Kronstadt. For several years the Swedish navy, that also had to fight against the strong Danish navy, managed to block the passage out of the Gulf of Finland for the Russians, but in 1714 Russian galleys manage to pass through the blockade and defeat a small Swedish squadron at Hangö in south-western Finland. The victory at Hangö is regarded as the birth moment of the Russian Baltic navy. From 1715 more and more Russian sailing ships began to operate in the Baltic Sea.

The Swedish navy, since 1680 based at Karlskrona, now also had to begin to construct an archipelago navy with rowing galleys in order to meet the threat from the Russian galleys, but it was too late to stop the devastating Russian attacks against Sweden's eastern coastline in 1719 but also in 1720–21.

During the first half of the war the navy had dominated the Baltic Sea, but during the 1710s it had to fight both the Danish and the growing Russian navy, and especially prevent them from coordinating their operations. It was an almost impossible mission, although the situation became a little easier in 1720, when a British naval force appeared in the Stockholm archipelago in order to prevent further Russian attacks.

The Final Struggle, 1718–21

At the beginning of 1716 Charles XII led an invading army into southern Norway, in an attempt to force Denmark out of the war. The Swedish army advanced towards Kristiania (Oslo) and began to besiege the fortress of Akershus. But lack of siege artillery and provisions forced the Swedes to cancel the whole operation and march back to Sweden.

The next two years were used to mobilise a new and larger army as well as large stores of provisions. The next invasion of Norway should not be hindered by lack of provisions. In the autumn the attack was launched. While the main army, commanded by the King himself, crossed the border in the south and began to besiege the fortress of Fredrikshald (Fredriksten), another army led by general Armfeldt advanced from Jämtland in Sweden into Tröndelagen in Norway with the aim to conquer Trondheim.

But this large invasion came to a sudden halt on 30 November 1718, when Charles XII was killed by a shot in the trench at Fredrikshald. The day after the King's death the leading generals held a conference at a meeting in Tistedalen, and decided to stop the siege immediately and withdraw the army back to Sweden. This fast decision has by some historians been seen as an indication that the King was killed after an assassination conspiracy. A majority, however, stress that ballistic examinations indicate that the shot

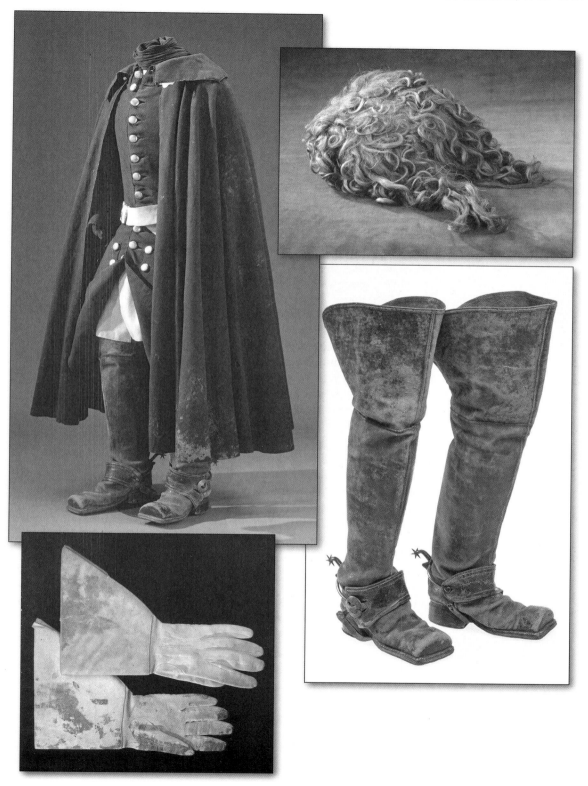

that killed the King came from the Norwegian positions and not from behind him. However, the invasion came to a halt, the army was withdrawn to Sweden, and in the north Armfeldt's army also left Norway. But the northern army was struck with disaster during its retreat, when it was caught by a snowstorm and some 3,000 men froze to death.

On 2 December 1718 Görtz was arrested in Bohuslän, close to the Norwegian border. In Stockholm in January 1719 Charles' sister Ulrika Eleonora was elected Queen of Sweden, and promised to abolish the royal autocracy, introduced by Charles XI in the early 1680s. Now the parliament regained much of its previous power. As a brutal symbol of the break with the old regime, Görtz was executed in Stockholm in February 1719. As a last step, in March 1720 Ulrika Eleonora's husband, Friedrich of Hessen, was elected King Fredrik I.

These were dramatic changes but the war still continued. In the summer of 1719 a large Russian galley fleet commanded by General Admiral Apraksin devastated much of the archipelago in eastern Sweden, and in that desperate situation Sweden tried to forge closer ties with Great Britain. To facilitate a closer cooperation with London, Sweden during the autumn 1719 signed a peace treaty with Britain's ally Hannover and ceded Bremen-Verden to Hannover. After British mediation another peace was signed with Prussia, and Sweden seceded the southern part of Vorpommern with Stettin and the islands Usedom and Wollin to the Kurfürst in Berlin. However important parts of the German possessions were still in Swedish hands, although all of them had been occupied by enemy armies. In 1720 another peace was signed, now with Denmark, without any territorial losses, but Sweden had to agree to once again pay customs to Denmark when her ships passed through Öresund, and also stop supporting her ally Holstein-Gottorp.

Only Russia was left in the war, but it was of course the most powerful enemy. Although the British Royal navy had entered the waters outside Stockholm in 1720 in order to prevent any new Russian attacks in the region, other Russian galley forces burned along the coastline of northern Sweden both in 1720 and 1721.

However in August 1721 it was finally over, after 21 years of war. Sweden signed a peace treaty with Russia in Nystad and ceded large territories: Estonia, Livonia, Ingria, a part of Karelia and south-eastern Finland including the city of Viborg as well as the two islands Ösel and Dagö (Hiiumaa). Two decades of war were over, and with them the Swedish empire. In its place Russia had established herself as the new great power in the Baltic Sea region.

The Costs of the War

The Great Northern War varied in intensity, but the Swedish army and navy were more or less mobilised for these two decades. Despite that the war must have been experienced as rather distant by many Swedes, especially during the years before Poltava. If a family was not hurt by the human losses the war might very well not have been present in the every day life of ordinary Swedes.

But from 1710 that definitively changed, with demands for more and more men in the army and numerous extra taxes. More and more men were killed, and thousands of refugees arrived from the eastern part of the realm. Then for those who lived in the archipelago came the terrible summer of 1719.

Regardless of how you exactly estimate the degree of fatigue in Sweden when peace came in 1721, it was without any doubt a nation which had been hit by severe blows. The Baltic provinces, Finland, Wismar, Bremen-Verden and Pomerania were all occupied and 1,250,000 of the Kingdom's inhabitants were under foreign occupation. In the western parts of Sweden about one million inhabitants remained. In Denmark and Russia thousands of POWs and also many civilian prisoners were in captivity, and many had been there for a decade.

Even though at the end of the war Sweden could still muster a rather impressive army and navy, there is no doubt that the country was close to a collapse. Between 1700 and 1721 around 200,000 soldiers had been killed, of whom about 50,000 came from Finland. Of all the men born between 1665 and 1702, i.e. the age groups that had to bear the main burden of the war effort, between one in three and one in four was killed in the service of the army and the navy.

It is not a surprise that Sweden at the end of the war had an excess of women, although it is very difficult to give exact figures. With that background the important question is not why the Swedish empire collapsed, rather how could it last so long? This makes the 1710s more and more interesting for the historian on the hunt for an answer as to how the Swedish "military state" was developed, in order to be able to stand total war in the modern sense of the word.

8

Battlefield Performance

During 21 years of war the Swedish army performed many campaigns, fought numerous battles, conquered or lost fortresses. Some of the battles were, of course, more important than others, while some were of more temporary importance. Here I have chosen six battles and one campaign to illustrate how the Swedish army worked in the field, at different times of the war. Despite what exactly was stipulated in regulations and books on military theory, the tactical behaviour of course differed depending on the actual situation at hand, the opponent, and the high command of the Swedish forces in that specific battle. One should also remember that many of the officers during the end of the war were just small children when the war broke out. The Carolean army of course changed and developed during these two decades. All this is of course certain, but still has to be acknowledged, and yet, the following examples show that there were some fundamentals in the army's tactical behaviour that were valid throughout the war.

Narva, 1700

The Russian attack against Sweden in 1700 began when Tsar Peter I commanded a large Russian army that started to besiege the Swedish town and fortress of Narva, on the border between the two Swedish provinces of Estonia and Ingria. The city had for a long time been a strategic commercial and fortress town connected via the river Narva to the southern shore of the Gulf of Finland just a few kilometres to the north. The town had been conquered by the Swedes from the Russians in 1581 and formally become Swedish in 1595.

In September 1700 37,000 Russian soldiers started the siege and at the same time built defensive field works in the opposite direction, to be able to meet and repel any Swedish attempt to rescue the besieged. Narva was defended by a garrison under the command of Colonel Henning Rudolf Horn, and would not have a chance to resist if no form of rescue arrived.

Swedish troops commanded by Charles XII landed in the Estonian harbour of Pernau and started a march towards the north-west. In early November about 10,000 Swedish soldiers had reached Wesenberg (Rakvere), about 100 kilometres from Narva. But the logistical difficulties were large. Winter was approaching and the feeding of men and horses became more and more

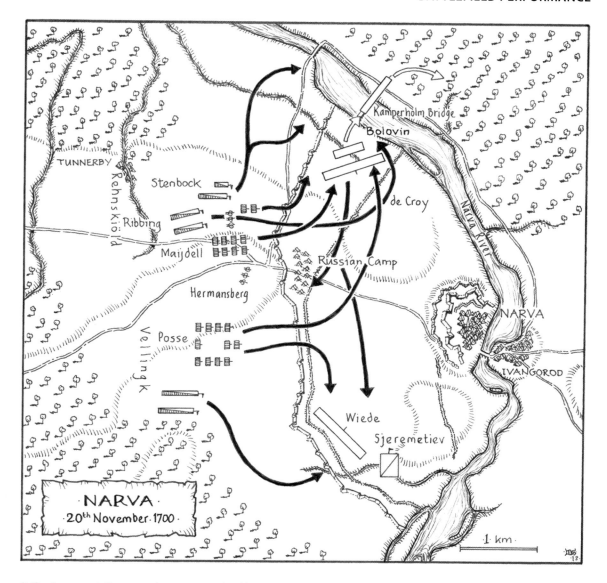

TUNNERBY

Rehnskiöld

Stenbock

Ribbing

Maijdell

Hermansberg

Vellingk

Posse

Kamperholm Bridge

Bolovin

de Croy

Russian Camp

Narva River

NARVA

IVANGOROD

Wiede

Sjeremetiev

NARVA
· 20th November · 1700 ·

1 km

difficult, especially since the Russians had burned large areas along the road to Narva, in order to prevent provisioning opportunities for the Swedes.

The most important factor now was time. If Narva could be rescued at all, that had to be very soon, before the defenders had to surrender. The field army would also begin to starve if it stayed at Wesenberg and did not move to regions with good stores. The problem was that the only secure stores, on Swedish controlled soil, were in western Estonia, while Narva was further to the east. Outside Narva were the Russian army's supplies which in case of a Swedish victory might by used by the Swedish army; however, more likely was a Swedish defeat outside Narva. There was one more alternative: to stay in Wesenberg, half starving, and wait for Swedish reinforcements with fresh supplies, but by the time they arrived the garrison at Narva would have surrendered.

In that situation Charles XII choose to advance towards Narva as fast as possible. On 13 November the army left Wesenberg and four days later drove away a smaller Russian force under Boris Sjeremetjev at Pyhäjoggi. It was more of a minor skirmish but boosted the morale of the Swedish army. On 19 November the advancing army was 14 kilometres from Narva and fired rockets and a Swedish 'password' signal with their guns, all to signal hope for Nava's garrison.

The Russians were convinced that the relatively weak Swedish army would not dare to attack before reinforcements had arrived. Tsar Peter left the Russian camp to ensure that the Russians would also get reinforcements. The commander-in-chief then became Field Marshal the Duke Charles Eugène de Croy, a Dutch officer of French origin. On paper his position was comfortable: 33,000 soldiers, of whom 26,000 were placed so they guarded the front towards the Swedish rescue army. They stood behind a 2.5 metre high embankment reinforced with 140 guns and a large number of chevaux-de-frise as storm barriers.

Charles XII could only muster 10,200 men, but for him there were no longer any alternatives, time was running out. General Carl Gustaf Rehnskiöld made a plan, both simple and easy, based upon local superiority. The Swedish army should be concentrated on one given point along the Russian defence line.

The Swedish soldiers had not been given any bread for four days and not been given anything to eat the last day. To make the attack easier, despite the winter weather they left their coats in the army camp together with their knapsacks. Before the attack, the Swedish artillery bombarded the Russian positions, followed by two signal rockets that were fired to tell Narva's garrison that the attack had begun.

In two columns the Swedish army advanced towards the Russian defence embankment while the cavalry covered the flanks, and was ready to repel any Russian attempts to counterattack. Just as the attack started a snow-blown hail began to drive directly into the eyes of the Russians, so they could not determine the distance to the Swedes, which is why the Russian guns kept quiet.

At a distance of 30 metres the first Swedes shot a musket fusillade and hand grenades were thrown, which checked the defenders. Immediately the Swedish force attacked with swords and bayonets, and the chevaux-de-frise were thrown away with the use of the swords. After a short while the Russian front was divided into three parts by the two attacking columns, and both of the columns turned to the left when they had broken through. While the snow kept falling the Russian right wing was driven towards the river Narva, while the cavalry was now concentrated against the Russian left wing, so the forces there were not given the opportunity to understand what happened to their comrades on the right.

Now thousands of Russian soldiers fled in panic towards the river and a pontoon bridge over to the eastern side of the river, the Kamperholms Bridge, but it collapsed under the pressure of thousands of fleeing men. The chaos developed further with thousands of Russian soldiers drowning in the ice-cold Narva river, while others took the opportunity to kill hated foreign officers.

At the end of the afternoon, after only three hours of battle, what remained of the Russian centre and the right wing were torn to pieces and

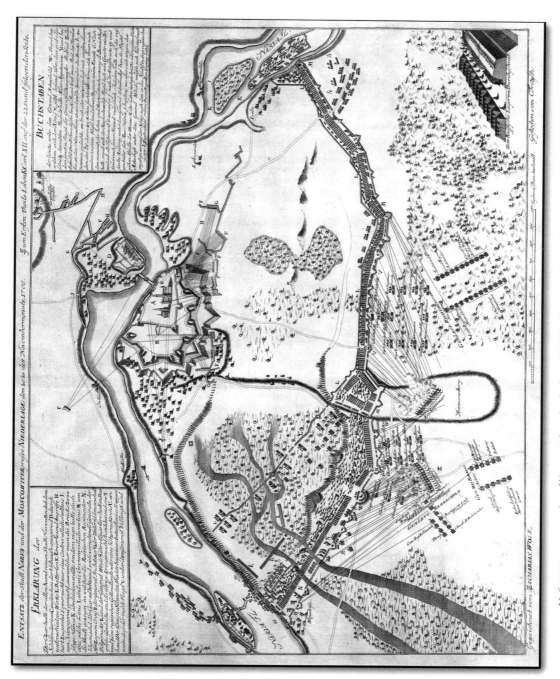

16. German map engraving of Narva, attributed to Zacharias Wolf. The illustration depicts the assault on the Russian siege lines.

in full chaos. In that situation de Croy chose to surrender, but despite that a minor part of the Russian right wing still fought from a carriage park close to the Kamperholms Bridge, and did not surrender until eight o'clock in the evening. Even worse: the Russian left wing was still intact, and there were some of the best regiments of the Russian army.

However, the night passed without any larger fighting; not least the Swedes were far too tired to be able to continue the struggle. Also many hungry Swedish soldiers had begun to plunder the Russian provisions and it was not only food that was swallowed. Drunken Swedish soldiers caused a lot of confusion during the night and there was some shooting by mistake between Swedish units, resulting in casualties due to friendly fire. In that situation a determined counterattack by the Russian left wing could have resulted in a disaster. But such an attack was never performed; the Swedes still had luck on their side. Instead the Russian left wing surrendered at two o'clock in the morning.

The Swedish victory was total. An army just about a third of the size of the enemy had won an enormous victory. Not only was the siege of Narva broken but also the main Russian army was destroyed. Russian casualties are difficult to estimate, but somewhere between 6,000 and 18,000 men were killed or drowned. At least 4,000 Russian cavalry managed to escape over the river before the bridge collapsed. The destiny for the remaining 10,000–20,000 Russian soldiers is uncertain, but many of them became POWs. The Swedish losses were 900 killed and 1,200 wounded.

Large numbers of field signs and arms (particularly guns) were taken by the Swedes, while the highest-ranking Russian officers had to go into Swedish captivity. But thousands of ordinary Russian soldiers were simply let loose, since the Swedes could not handle so many prisoners. Instead the Swedish army went into a winter camp at Lais in eastern Estonia.

In later Swedish tales about the battle it is sometimes said that the Russian army counted 100,000 men, figures that are extremely exaggerated. It resulted in a tradition of how "one against ten fought" (in a famous poem of 1818) and won that wonderful victory. It was an enormous victory at Narva in November 1700, although not that enormous. Narva was one of the Swedish army's greatest victories ever, won with an offensive tactic that totally surprised the enemy, and also with some help of the weather that made large parts of the Russian army blind to what happened around them.

Fraustadt, 1706

The Swedish victory over a Saxon-Polish army at Fraustadt (Wschowa in south-western Poland) was in older Swedish history writing, especially during the 1910s, used as a a scholarly example of the classic tactic to surround and destroy the enemy, inspired by Hannibal and the Carthaginians' victory against the Romans at Cannae in 216 B.C. Today historians agree that it was an important victory, but hardly based upon historical knowledge about Hannibal's victory over the Romans during antiquity. Instead it is regarded as the obvious result of sound tactical thinking and excellent military leadership, which is of course important enough.

Around the New Year 1705–06 large Polish and Russian forces were concentrated in eastern Poland, while the main Saxon army was in the west, in Saxony. For the Swedes it was crucial to prevent these two armies meeting and joining forces. In order to do so the Swedish army had to strike fast first in one direction and then in the other. But the allies forced them into a much more risky operation.

The Swedish main army of 20,000 men under Charles XII besieged about 26,000 united Saxon-Polish-Russian soldiers at Grodno in the east, and everyone expected the decisive battle to occur there. But instead the allies chose to try to annihilate a smaller Swedish army, 10,000 strong, under the command of the cavalry general Carl Gustaf Rehnskiöld in western Poland. After that they would join forces with the allied army at Grodno and together destroy Charles XII's main army.

With that ambition the Saxon lieutenant general Johann Matthias von der Schulenburg in January 1706 led an army from Saxony towards the east. The commanded the Saxon main army reinforced with some Russian units, in total 18,300 men. But the presumed target, the general Rehnskiöld, did not sit still waiting to be attacked, neither did he retreat. On the contrary he advanced towards the enemy, despite his army being just half as strong as Schulenburg's forces at only 9,400 men.

On 3 February 1706 the two armies moved towards each other at Fraustradt in western Poland. Over half of the Swedes, 5,700, were cavalry, while the rest were infantry. Schulenburg commanded 19 Saxon and 10 Russian infantry battalions, a little more than 16,000 men. But his cavalry was weak, only 2,000 men. In total the allies could muster 18,300 men. For Rehnskiöld the only hope for success was to use his superiority in cavalry as much as possible. On the other hand Schulenburg had to rely on his superiority in infantry, almost three to one. That is why two very different battle plans took form.

Schulenburg's army managed to take a very good defensive position, behind a forest and alongside a stream and marches, a position that forced any advancing Swedish force to move directly towards the strong Saxon-Russian infantry positions. He knew that the Swedes regarded the Russian units for being of lesser quality than the Saxon, which they were very right to. He did not want the Swedes to concentrate an attack against the weaker Russian positions. So, just to be sure, he ordered the Russian soldiers to turn their green uniforms inside out, so that their red lining should make the Swedes believe that all the mass of infantry units were Saxons.

Rehnskiöld's plan was both simple and difficult: his centre was filled with infantry, with cavalry on the both wings. Together they would launch a frontal attack against the enemy, the terrain would hardly allow anything else. Despite its inferiority his infantry centre had the task of engaging the enemy's main force without allowing it to break through. At the same time the cavalry wings would attack the enemy wings and defeat the Saxon cavalry, before they would turn around and ("attack the infantry in its back"). Then the enemy infantry would be squeezed. To camouflage his intentions Rehnskiöld held back his cavalry during the first moments of the battle.

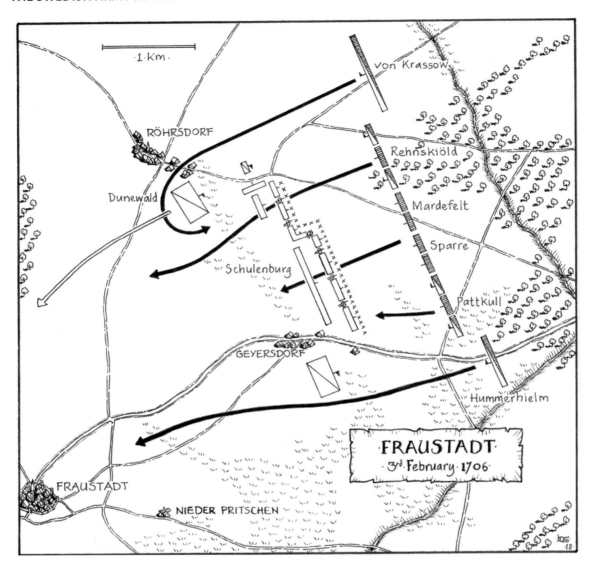

Around noon the Swedes began their advance towards the enemy positions. Very soon the cavalry had advanced faster than the infantry in the centre. On the left wing some of the marches had frozen so the Swedish cavalry could easily ride across. But the Swedish horses had no horseshoes, so many of the horses were "[slipping] upon the ice so most of the regiment stumbled", as one regimental commander later said. Saxon counterattacks with cavalry were not able to stop the Swedish charge and soon all Saxon cavalry had fled.

The Swedish centre was hit by three fusillades from the guns, the last one with canisters, but still they had managed to open a small breach in the Saxon lines, broad enough that Swedish cavalry could attack into it. At the same time Swedish cavalry circled into the back of the enemy. The Russian infantry to the left was under such a hard pressure that it could no longer fight in a disciplined manner. In order to avoid a collapse Schulenburg sent two Saxon battalions and one battalion of French grenadiers into the centre, where infantry from Kronoberg's and Västmanland's regiments pressed hard.

But the French battalion was not so eager to die for the Saxons, and soon gave up the fight, and the whole Saxon centre began to pull back. On the right wing the Saxon guard fired and caused large casualties among Västerbotten's infantry regiment. Another Saxon battalion and a Swiss battalion fought hard when Nyland's cavalry regiment pressed upon them. But despite these stronger positions the whole Saxon army now began to withdraw.

The Russian infantry was crushed and the remaining Saxon infantry soon became surrounded and had to surrender. Schulenburg himself had been hit in his right hip, but managed to escape. Only minor parts of his army managed to escape, and on the battlefield lay

17. Carl Gustaf Rehnskiöld. A field marshal, his military skills made him the chief military adviser and second-in-command to the King. Following Poltava, he was held in captivity until 1718.

about 7,300 dead Saxon and Russian soldiers, while another 7,600 had been taken prisoner. The Swedish casualties are estimated to 400 killed and 740 wounded.

However, the Swedish victory was stained by events that occurred before the battle concluded. Several Swedes witnessed later how many surrendering Russians were slaughtered, partly for the reason that they were so many that they could not be taken care of. Later on there were accusations towards the Swedish high command, including Charles XII himself, that they had sanctioned mass murder on Russian prisoners, though there is no evidence for that. But Rehnskiöld, as commander-in-chief at Fraustadt, had to carry the responsibility for what happened, despite the fact that it is most uncertain how many Russians were killed.

Of the other prisoners three regiments of Saxons in Swedish service were formed, and they would play an important role in the battle at Helsingborg in 1710. Also other Germans as well as French and Swiss units were formed and put into the Swedish army.

Rehnskiöld has been celebrated for this victory, both during the war and the posterity. His plan had most probably not been inspired by the victory of Hannibal, but by Rehnskiöld's own tactical skill.

We should also remember that August II was only 120 kilometres away, in Kalisch, with 8,000 cavalry. If they managed to join forces with Schulenburg, then Rehnskiöld's last advantage, his large cavalry, would have disappeared.

So Rehnskiöld was in a hurry. His large victory meant that Saxony now was opened for a Swedish invasion and on September 14 1706 a peace treaty was signed at Altranstädt. August and Saxony were forced to leave the war, although they came back in full force in the summer of 1709. But the Altranstädt peace opened a window of opportunity for Charles XII and the Swedes, namely to concentrate upon the only enemy left. In August 1707 the Swedish army left its bases in Saxony for the long march east and the invasion of Russia.

Poltava, 1709

The battle at Poltava is the most famous, and also most devastating, that the Carolean army fought. The invasion of Russia aimed to tempt the Russian main army to a decisive battle, so it could be destroyed. The Narva victory would be repeated and result in a final victory in the war.

But the Russian army avoided that decisive battle and used the 'scorched earth' tactic to make provisions more and more difficult for the advancing Swedes, the deeper into Russia they went. On September 29, 1708 an army corps with a large provision column aimed for the main army was crushed by the Russians at Lesjnaja. Peter the Great later called Lesjnaja "the victory's mother", the battle that laid the ground for Poltava.

In that situation Charles XII turned south towards the Ukraine, to find food and winter quarters for his army, but also to join anti-Russian Cossacks. Probably was his plan to advance towards the north-east, over Charkov (Charkiv), and up to Moscow the next year. But instead the Russian army followed the Swedes into the Ukraine, and in the spring and early summer of 1709 the both sides manoeuvred to get the best positions. Regardless of whether the Swedes intended to advance towards Moscow or retreat back to Poland, they had to secure a crossing over the River Vorskla. At that very spot lay the city of Poltava, held by a Russian garrison. The Swedes also thought that there were substantial Russian provisions inside Poltava. So on 1 May 1709 the Swedish army started a siege of Poltava.

But the siege became protracted and on the night of 16 June the Russian main army under the command of Tsar Peter arrived, began to cross Vorskla and began to built a fortified camp about 10 kilometres north of Poltava. With that move, the Russians blocked the way towards the north for the Swedes. Charles XII hade made several attempts to persuade the Ottoman Sultan Ahmed III and his ally the Khan of Crimea to join forces with the Swedes, but without any success. That meant that also the southern route from Poltava, into the territories controlled by the Turks or the Khan was closed. In that situation the only alternative left for Charles and his army was to fight the Russians.

The Swedish army of a little more than 20,000 and their allied Zaporog Cossacks under Mazepa faced an overwhelming army of 53,000 Russian soldiers, of whom 4,000 were in the Poltava garrison. The only alternative for the Swedes was a swift and surprising attack, a protracted action would certainly lead to disaster. Since Charles XII had been injured by a shot in his foot, the plan was formed by General Carl Gustaf Rehnskiöld. The Russians had built six redoubts ahead of their main camp, and Rehnskiöld's plan was to overrun and bypass these redoubts when it still was dark, so that he then could launch a surprise attack against the Russian camp. The plan has

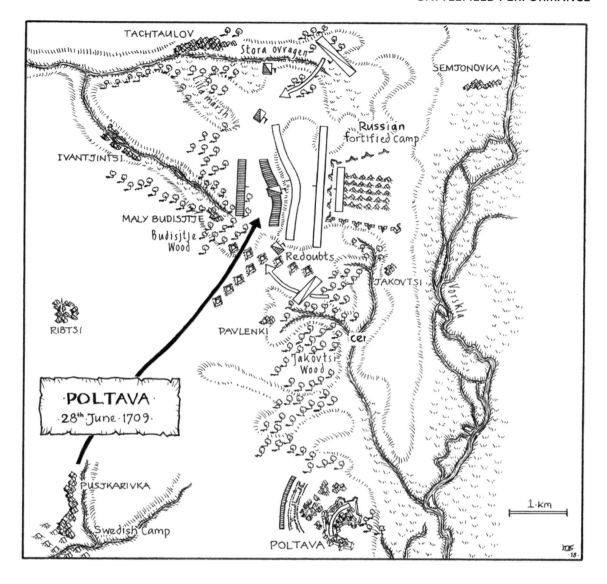

obvious similarities with the successful plan at Narva nine years earlier, a plan that Rehnskiöld also had been responsible for.

At midnight on 28 June the Swedish infantry, 8,200 strong, began to advance in four columns, under the command of General Adam Lewenhaupt. With them followed Charles XII himself, borne on a stretcher and escorted by 24 men of the Lifeguard. After them followed Major Generals Carl Gustaf Creutz and Hugo Johan Hamilton with 7,800 men cavalry in six columns. In the Swedish army camp at the village Pusjkarivka 2,000 sick and wounded were left. For the protection of the camp and the route along the River Vorskla another 5,000 men were detached. Besides that, 3,000 Zaporozhian Cossacks were left in the camp, and a Walachian regiment of light Polish cavalry of 1,100 men had been sent away to scout on the Russian camp and if necessary draw the enemy's attention.

18. Clockwise from left: career officer Carl Gustaf Roos, who had served Charles XII's father; Ukrainian 'hetman' Ivan Mazepa (18th century German engraving, attributed to Daniel Bayle); Axel Gyllenkrok, quartermaster to the King's army (portrait attributed to Georg Engelhard Schröder); General Adam Lewenhaupt (lithograph after David von Krafft).

To make the army as mobile as possible the main part of the artillery was left in the camp, and only four light 3-pound guns were brought with the advancing troops. With that decision the Swedes lost any capability of heavier bombardment, but everything was gambled on speed and surprise.

At about half past two on the morning on 29 June the units were grouped for attack. But at the same time scouts had discovered that the Russians during the night had built another four redoubts at a right angle towards the earlier six. The Russian redoubts formed a large "T" that could split the Swedish columns and also expose them to fire from the flanks. But regardless of these obstacles, the redoubt system had to be bypassed if the army was to reach the Russian camp, the main target of the attack.

In the absence of the wounded Charles XII, Rehnskiöld and Lewenhaupt disagreed over the best tactic, and valuable time was lost while they were arguing. It was not until four o'clock in the morning that the Swedes were ready to attack, by then the sun already had risen and the Swedish army was clearly visible from the Russian positions. The 10 redoubts were defended by 4,000 Russian soldiers and behind them waited 9,000 men cavalry under General Mensjikov, while also the Russian camp now was alarmed and began to prepare for battle.

Now there was hardly any alternative left for the Swedes, but to make the best of the situation. One problem was that several officers lacked insight into the battle plan, i.e. that the Russian camp was the main objective. Instead they concentrated too much force attacking the redoubts instead of looking for possibilities to bypass them. Two redoubts were taken, before Major General Carl Gustaf Roos with his column became stuck in its attempt to conquer the third. Now Roos' force was attacked also by other Russian units, and took cover in a deserted redoubt. At about nine o'clock in the morning Roos had to surrender when only 400 of his 2,600 men were able to continue the fight.

Without the knowledge of Roos the rest of the Swedish infantry had managed to break through the redoubt line, while the Swedish cavalry led by Rehnskiöld drove away and pursued the Russian cavalry. But when he feared to get too far from his own infantry, Rehnskiöld interrupted the persecution, and involuntarily gave the Russian cavalry a possibility to reunite with the Russian main force. This decision has been very much criticised, but the question is whether Rehnskiöld had any choice, since the attack force of the Swedish cavalry began to fade away, and it also was shot at by Russian guns.

But much worse was that also the infantry, under the command of Lewenhaupt, had been called back from an attempt to break into the Russian camp. Rehnskiöld, as supreme commander, wanted to gather all his forces before it was time to launch a massive attack against it. For this reason he then spent two hours in a fruitless search for Roos' "lost" infantry column.

IOHANNES
MAZEPPA
Cosaccorum Zaporo
viensium Supremus
Belli Dux

All this time was used by the Russians to prepare for what was to come. They lined up along a two kilometre-long front, two lines deep. In the centre there were 42 battalions infantry or 22,000 men, and on the wings 59 squadrons of cavalry or 13,800 men. Among the Russian units 70 light field guns had been placed. In connection with that it is worth remembering that almost all the Swedish artillery had been left behind, and the four small guns the army brought with it had now been left at the Russian redoubts.

The Swedish infantry was hopelessly inferior, and to make the situation even worse, one unit, Västmanland's Regiment, had been sent away to search for Roos' missing column. When the moment for the final part of the battle came around 10 o'clock in the morning no one in the Swedish command knew that Roos' men since about an hour into the battle had been in Russian captivity.

What followed was a development that could hardly could end in more than one way. Against the Russian centre's 22,000 men now stood only 10 Swedish infantry battalions, about one Swede against every four Russians. But instead of trying to escape, the Swedes chose to attack. It was obviously a lack of appreciation of the enemy, and a fatal one. Tsar Peter's army of 1709 was of a totally different and much higher quality than it had been in 1700.

The Swedish soldiers were forbidden to shoot with their muskets until they were almost upon the enemy, and could literally see the whites of his eyes. During the 800 metre long march towards the Russian line the officers and men from the Lifeguard, Uppland's, Kalmar, Östgöta, Närke-Värmland's and Skaraborg's infantry regiments were exposed to a terrible fire from the Russian artillery and after a while also from the Russians' muskets.

The Russian right wing was pressed on retreat and a handful of guns were captured, but parts of the Swedish battle line could not hold the same pace as the rest, a gap opened in the line and Russian troops poured into it. Then discipline collapsed and the Swedish infantry began to run, while the cavalry made shocking counterattacks in order to cover the retreat of the infantry.

Only half an hour after the start of the final Swedish assault everything was over. Rehnskiöld and several other high ranking officers were taken prisoner by the Russians, while Charles XII at the very last minute was helped up on a horse and managed to ride away.

At least 6,900 Swedes had been killed and 2,800 became POWs, but there are historians that argue that maybe as many as 8,000–9,000 Swedes were killed. Regardless of the exact figures it was large disaster, and the price the Russians paid for their victory was relatively moderate: 1,345 killed and 3,190 wounded.

At around one o'clock in the afternoon the surviving Swedes began to reach their own camp at Pusjkarivka and at nightfall the Swedish army began their retreat. In relatively good order they left the camp and Poltava, and moved towards the south along Vorskla eagerly looking for a ford were they could cross the broad Dnjepr and march towards the south-west in an attempt to reach Turkish territory. But the Russians followed the Swedes and harassed them. A suggested ford at Perevolotjna could not be found. Instead the general quartermaster Axel Gyllenkrok recommended the King to turn to the east over Vorskla and try to reach the territory of the Khan of Crimea.

But the army was heading for Dnjepr, and at noon on 30 June unit after unit of the Swedish army arrived at Perevolotjna. With the Russians not far

Uniform Plates by Sergey Shamenkov

Plate 1

(L–R): General, staff officer and Charles XII

(Illustration by Sergey Shamenkov, © Helion & Company)

See Colour Plate Commentaries for further information.

Plate 2

'Elite Cavalry' (L–R): Private of Life Dragoons, Trooper of Life Regiment, Corporal Drabant

(Illustration by Sergey Shamenkov, © Helion & Company)

See Colour Plate Commentaries for further information.

Plate 3

'Elite Infantry' (L–R): Guards Regiment Lifeguard officer, pikeman and musketeer
(Illustration by Sergey Shamenkov, © Helion & Company)
See Colour Plate Commentaries for further information.

Plate 4

'Elite Infantry': Grenadier, close up details of equipment and various styles of grenadier cap (not worn on campaign)

(Illustration by Sergey Shamenkov, © Helion & Company)

See Colour Plate Commentaries for further information.

Plate 5

**Line infantry regiment: musician, pikeman, officer.
For example Dal or Uppland regiments.**

(Illustration by Sergey Shamenkov, © Helion & Company)

See Colour Plate Commentaries for further information.

Plate 6

**Line infantry regiment: pikeman, officer, musketeer.
For example, Närke-Värmland or Nyland regiments.**

(Illustration by Sergey Shamenkov, © Helion & Company)

See Colour Plate Commentaries for further information.

Plate 7

**Line cavalry regiment: for example, Nyland, Småland,
Åbo & Björneborg regiments**

(Illustration by Sergey Shamenkov, © Helion & Company)

See Colour Plate Commentaries for further information.

Plate 8

Artillery: officer, two 'other ranks'

(Illustration by Sergey Shamenkov, © Helion & Company)

See Colour Plate Commentaries for further information.

Flags – Graphic Reconstructions by Lesley Prince

From original drawings in the Swedish War Archive collection

A)

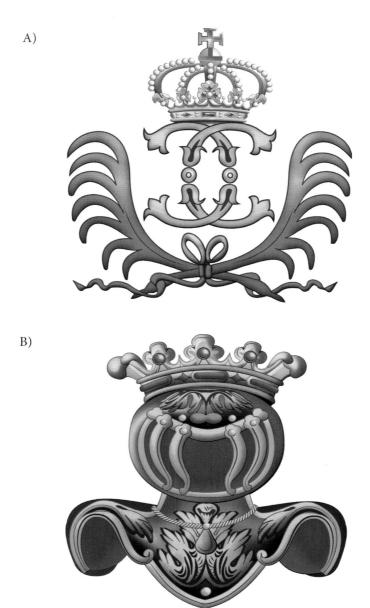

B)

A) Cipher of Charles XII, c.1700
B) Swedish helm c.1700

C)

D)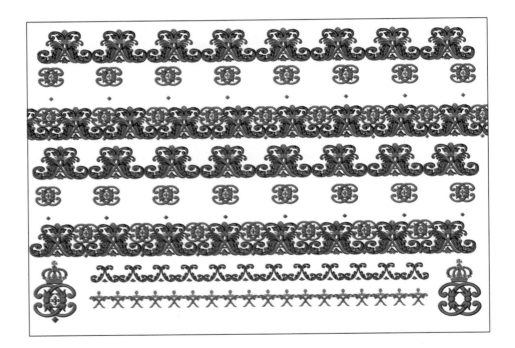

C) Swedish helm c.1700, pierced
D) Swedish border

Colours and Standards According to the Regulation of 1686

Björneborg infantry
regiment company colour

Carelia and Viborg
cavalry regiment

Dal regiment
company colour

Österbotten infantry
regiment company colour

Skaraborg infantry regiment
company colour

Södermanland infantry
regiment company colour

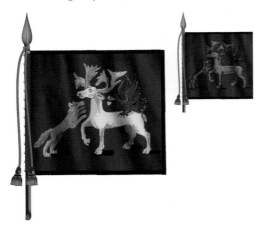

Jämtland cavalry company
obverse

Jämtland cavalry company
reverse

Life Regiment of Horse
Colonel's colour

Life Regiment of Horse
Närke company

Nylands och Tavestehus
cavalry regiment obverse

Nylands och Tavestehus
cavalry regiment reverse

Småland cavalry obverse

Småland cavalry reverse

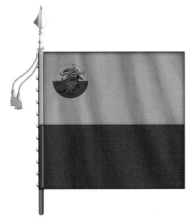

Östra (Eastern) Skånska
Conscripted Regiment company
colour (post-1686 Regulation)

Uppland 3-männing Cavalry
Regiment 1700 Östgöta company
standard (post-1686 Regulation)

Uniform Colours

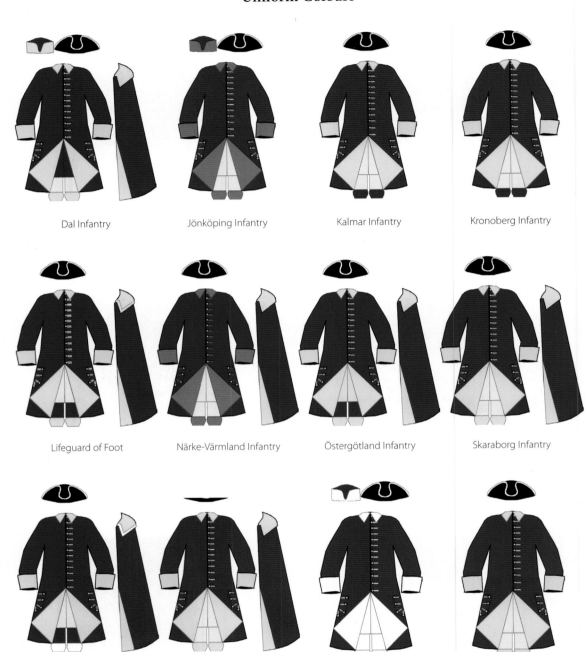

Dal Infantry

Jönköping Infantry

Kalmar Infantry

Kronoberg Infantry

Lifeguard of Foot

Närke-Värmland Infantry

Östergötland Infantry

Skaraborg Infantry

Södermanland Infantry

Uppland Infantry

Västerbotten Infantry

Västmanland Infantry

Illustrations by David Wright, © Helion & Company 2018

Åbo & Björneborg Cavalry   Drabant Cavalry   Karelska Cavalry   Life Regiment of Horse

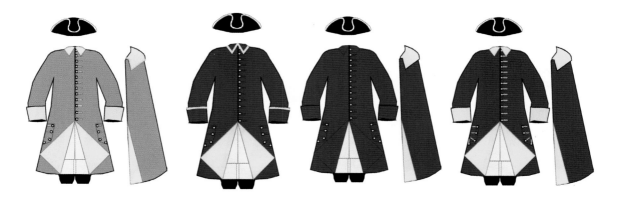

Livonian Nobility Banner   Northern Scanian Cavalry   Nyland Cavalry   Östgöta Cavalry

Småland Cavalry   Southern Scanian Cavalry   Swedish Nobility Banner   Uppland Cavalry

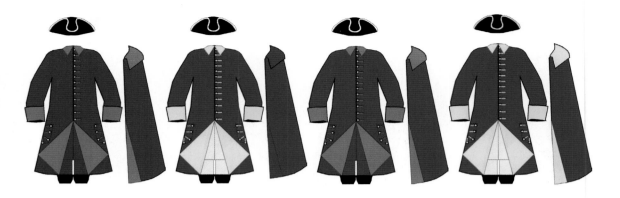

D'Albedyhl Dragoons   Dücker Dragoons   Gyllenstierna Dragoons   Hielm Dragoons

Life Dragoons   Meijerfelt Dragoons   Schlippenbach Dragoons   Schreiterfeldt Dragoons

Skånska (Scanian) Stånds-dragoons   Taube Dragoons   Uppland Stånds-Dragoons   Artillery

away the commanding generals managed to convince Charles XII to cross the Dnjepr, which he did together with the Cossack hetman Mazepa and about 1,000 men.

However the rest of the army was trapped, and on 1 July Lewenhaupt decided to surrender. That was a decision that has been much debated by generations of historians, but it was clear that the army was exhausted and demoralised. A continued struggle would most likely have resulted in a slaughter. The 300 Zaporozhian Cossacks who did not manage to cross the Dnjepr were executed immediately, while the Swedes went into captivity.

In total the number of prisoners were 16,358 officers and soldiers, 4,843 civilian staff (priests, clerks, surgeons, craftsmen and labourers), and 1,647 women and children. They were taken to Moscow were they were the prime element during Peter's large victory parade. After that the prisoners were distributed to a number of places were they often had to work hard, and many succumbed: the building of St Petersburg, the shipyards at Voronezj, and prisoner colonies in Tobolsk and other places in Siberia. Few of the POWs were exchanged during the war, but most were released after the peace in 1721. It has been estimated that one out of four prisoners survived the long captivity. The last prisoner from Poltava came back home to Sweden in 1745, after 36 years in captivity.

Many of the decisions made by the leading Swedish generals during and immediately after the battle at Poltava have been criticised, or at least discussed, for generations, and some have meant that the absence of Charles XII as the supreme commander paved the way for the disaster. But at the same time one has realise that the Russian superiority was overwhelming, and the Tsar's army also had developed into a modern and well-disciplined war machine, while the Swedish army had suffered hard during the winter of 1708–09. The question is whether there was any possibility at all that the outcome could have been different under these circumstances?

When Charles XII had manage to escape into Turkish exile, he wrote to the government in Stockholm and stressed "that it is most necessary that one now not headlong lose the courage nor release the grip on the task, but with the ultimate force" try to repair the damage. In spite of the disaster new regiments should be recruited and a new army sent into field, that was the King's intention and so it would be. The 40,000 men that had left Saxony in the autumn of 1707 were gone, but the war would continue. Poltava was a disaster, but not the final act.

Helsingborg, 1710

Only a few months after the Poltava disaster, on 2 November 1709, a Danish army landed at Råå fishing village just south of Helsingborg in north-western Scania. Now was the time for Denmark to take back her lost provinces that had been taken by the Swedes in the peace treaties of 1645 and 1658.

Warning fires were lit along the coast of Scania, but there were hardly any ready units to meet the invaders. Instead Helsingborg fell into Danish hands after a few days and by early December large parts of Scania was under Danish control. Only the fortresses in Landskrona and Malmö at Öresund's coast were still hold by there Swedish garrisons, but they were hopelessly

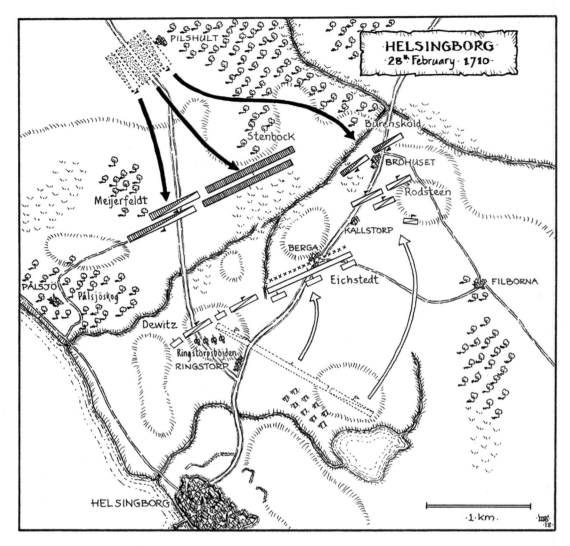

isolated when the Danish army advanced towards the north-east. After a minor skirmish outside Kristianstad on January 13, 1710 the last Swedish forced pulled out of Scania, towards the north. Very soon the Danish army stood outside Karlshamn in western Blekinge and it was obvious that they intended to advance towards Karlskrona, the main base of the Swedish navy.

When all this happened General Magnus Stenbock worked hard to raise another army to be able to confront the invading Danish army. The core of his new army was 60 companies of infantry from 20 different units, half of them veterans, the other half new recruits. In the historical tradition Magnus Stenbock's soldiers were called "goat boys", indicating that the army mostly consisted of young, inexperienced boys, but that was not the historical truth.

We can see how Stenbock's operational plan developed, when he founded almost a dozen field caches, mainly in northern Scania, as bases for the army operations. During February 1710 large amounts of provisions were delivered to Stenbock's army: bread, meat, pork, rye, grain, oats, wheat, salt,

19. Print depicting the battle of Battle of Helsingborg, 28 February 1710. Having been knocked out of the war in 1700, the Danes aimed to t take advantage of the Swedish defeat at Poltava to reclaim the lost province of Scania. Helsingborg was to mark their final failed attempt to regain them.

butter, cheese, beer, schnapps, hop, grouts, peas and tobacco. A large amount of provision also had to walk itself to the different regiments: 2,010 oxen, 95 steers, 116 young cattle for fattening and 25 sheep. Money was raised from the civilian administration in Scania, where Magnus Stenbock, practically enough, was also governor general.

In mid-February 1710 Stenbock did not dare wait any longer, since the Danish threat towards Karlskrona was too big. His army began to advance towards the south with 10 infantry and nine cavalry regiments. Of these 19 regiments 11 were newly organised, which of course meant that they were lacking drill and training. Especially among the lower officer ranks and the NCOs there were a lot of vacancies; far too many NCOs and officers had been killed during the campaign through Poland, Russia and the Ukraine, and they were not easy to replace in a short period of time. Besides that the army was also short of horses and uniforms, but an advantage was that it had plenty of ammunition.

For the Swedish army it was not only a question of repelling the Danish invasion, it had to be done with so few casualties that the army also could be used in Pomerania. The Swedish operational plan succeeded so far that the Danish army from its positions south of Kristianstad began to move towards the west, in order not to lose contact with Helsingborg and the connection with Denmark. When the Danish commander general Christian Detlev Reventlow fell sick he was replaced by Lieutenant General Jörgen Rantzau who was even more eager to keep the road open to Helsingborg. He feared being squeezed between Stenbock's army approaching from the north and the Swedish garrison in Malmö in the south. So, on 19 February, the Danes began their retreat towards Helsingborg, followed by Stenbock's army.

When Rantzau reached Helsingborg he was met by reinforcements that had been sent over Öresund, and as a result he could now muster 10,000 infantry and 4,000 cavalry, which he all concentrated just north of Helsingborg. On the night to 28 February Stenbock came to Flening, 10 kilometres east of Helsingborg, his army just about the same size as the Danish one, but with a larger proportion of cavalry.

The terrain between the two armies was filled with marshes, deep ditches and piles of stone, making it more or less impossible to keep the units together in battle formation. In order to avoid that terrain Stenbock's army early in the morning on 28 February marched to the west and at the village Allerum turned towards the south. When they were approaching the Danish army the Swedish units were divided into five columns. The plan was to strike against the left wing of the Danes, i.e. the units closest to Öresund, in order to cut off the enemy from all opporttunity to evacuate over to Zealand.

But during the early hours of that morning a thick fog made it difficult to see exactly who was where. When the fog lifted around 10 o'clock in the morning both sides were surprised to discover the real positions. Stenbock realised that the Danes had a more favourable position than he had assumed from the intelligence reports he had been given. For Rantzau it was a shock to realize that his left wing was in great danger, and if it collapsed his whole army could be cut of from Öresund. For the Danes it was crucial to grab and keep the initiative.

Rantzau immediately reinforced his left wing and also positioned artillery close to it, at Ringstorp hill, and at half past eleven the Danish artillery began to fire upon the Swedish positions. But then Stenbock made a surprise move. Instead of making use of his advantageous position on his right wing, he turned his whole army to the left, and suddenly a threat emerged against the Danish right wing. The Danes answered by letting their right wing advance towards the Swedes. That move was understandable, but gaps were opened in the previously well-prepared Danish lines.

But the Danes tried to take the initiative, and their right wing cavalry rode to the attack. They also managed to drive back Swedish cavalry but at the cost of many officers. Soon the Swedish left wing struck back and in order to prevent a Swedish breakthrough Rantzau went to his right wing. But by doing so he lost the possibility to lead his whole army, and after a short while he also was hit by a shot through one of his lungs.

In this situation the Danish formations began to dissolve. A false rumour was spread that Swedish cavalry was attacking in the Danish back, and soon the whole Danish right wing was trying to escape towards Helsingborg.

At the same time the infantry Swedish centre began to advance, shouting "With the help of God and Jesus". With the supporting fire from 34 guns the Swedes fired their muskets 30 steps away from the Danish line, and then attacked with bayonets and pikes. First the Danes were very well disciplined and fired several times against the advancing Swedes, but then they became aware that their right wing was routed. In that situation the lack of a supreme commander proved to be fatal. The Danish infantry tried to pull back, but as was often the case it was very difficult for a force to retreat in good order when it was engaged in battle. Two Danish elite units, the Grenadier Corps and the Guard of Foot, stood steady and stopped the Swedes, so that the main part of the Danish right wing could withdraw. The casualties were severe on both sides. Småland's three- and four-männing regiment directly attacked the Danish guard, and lost 200 of its 550 men. At the same time Swedish cavalry managed to ride through the Danish lines, and began to chase and cut down fleeing Danish soldiers.

On the Danish left wing another gap had opened in the line, and also here Swedish cavalry began to ride through. Also Major General Frantz Joachim von Dewitz, commander of the left wing, had been sent to the exposed right wing, and therefore there was no higher officer that could coordinate the movements of the right wing.

A Hungarian dragoon regiment in Danish service tried to fill the gap between the left wing and the centre, but was driven back by Swedish cavalry and fled towards Helsingborg. The pressure on the two remaining Danish regiments in the centre became harder by the minute under attacks from Uppland's Regiment and a Saxon regiment in Swedish service, and in order to avoid their erasure, the Grenadier Corps and the Guard of Foot as well as all other Danish units that still stood on the battlefield were ordered to retreat.

Thanks to the short distance to Helsingborg the remaining Danish infantry managed to save themselves in the town. Although minor skirmishes continued for the rest of the day, the battle was over, and Stenbock assembled his army on the place where the Danish camp had been. He was very well aware of his task to save Scania, but to do it without risking larger casualties, so an assault on Helsingborg was out of the question. The battle had cost the Swedish army 3,000 killed or wounded, but the Danish casualties were about 5,000 with another 2,500 taken prisoner. The Danes had also lost their artillery and with the Swedish army waiting outside Helsingborg there could only be one decision for the new Danish commander, Major General von Dewitz.

On 5 March 1710 the remnants of the Danish army left Helsingborg without a fight and the men were shipped the short distance over to Helsingör, but the Danes left a terrible trace of themselves behind. They had no opportunity to evacuate their horses and had no intention of leaving them to the Swedes. No fewer than 5,000 Danish army horses were shot in the streets, then were cut up and their remains dragged into cellars and kitchens, or thrown down into wells while intestines poured out of the bodies. Into this mess about 10,000 barrels of grain, peas and salt were dumped. The 22 iron guns that remained in the town were nailed and the powder stretched out.

The sight that met the Swedish soldiers, not to mention the civilian inhabitants of Helsingborg, must have been indescribable. Although it was the middle of the winter and not the hottest part of the summer, it was still very urgent to clean the town, but both soldiers and civilians refused to deal with the dead horses. Handling dead animals was a task for the most despised persons. But not all of those in the whole of Sweden and Denmark would be enough to solve this problem, so the Swedish army had to force farmers and fishermen from the areas around Helsingborg to come and dig mass graves in the frozen earth and clean the town. Some of these horse graves have been excavated and many horses were buried with saddles, bridles and other equipment, no effort had been spent to take care of them, the gravediggers were obviously in a hurry and the task too overwhelming.

Historians used to see Swedish tactics as more offensive Swedish compared to the Danish, but modern historians see little difference. We can also see that the Swedish army, for the Carolean epoch, used a lot of field artillery. The battle ended with a clear Swedish victory, due to the fact that Stenbock was flexible enough to use the gaps that developed in the Danish lines. When Rantzau and several high-ranking Danish officers were then concentrated on their right wing, supreme command over the Danish army was lost and the whole command structure crumbled, with a fatal result for the Danes.

Magnus Stenbock had won a decisive Swedish victory and retaken Scania, which was important enough, and at a relatively small cost. It was an important success. But almost half of the Danish army remained on Zealand, although without its artillery and horses, and that meant a potential threat against Scania still existed.

Gadebusch, 1712

In 1712 Danish, Saxon and Russian forces had conquered large parts of the Swedish provinces in northern Germany. The city of Stade, close to Bremen, was in Danish hands and other Danish forces besieged Wismar, while a Saxon–Russian army besieged Stettin in the east; the important city of Stralsund was surrounded by forces from all three enemies. In the waters outside Pomerania Danish naval ships were sailing in order to cut the lines

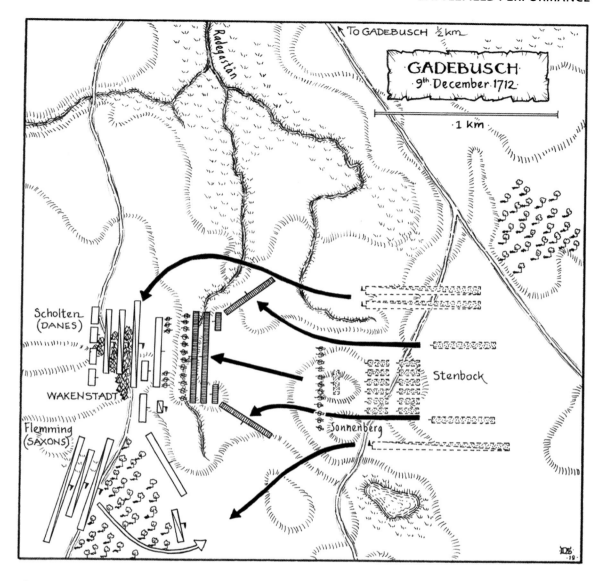

of sea communications between Sweden and her German territories.

At that time Charles XII was still in exile in Bender, Turkey. But the King demanded that a Swedish army should be transported to Pomerania, defeating the enemies there, and then be ready to march through eastern Europe to the Ottoman Empire. Only if he could contribute with an army of his own, would Charles be able to convince the Sultan in Constantinople to join forces with the Swedes in a joint invasion of Russia. It might seem a very unrealistic plan, but on the other hand what were the alternatives for Charles XII if he wanted to crush Peter and thwart the defeat at Poltava?

After large mobilisation efforts in Sweden a Swedish army under the command of Magnus Stenbock, the winner at Helsingborg 1710, landed at Rügen in Pomerania on September 16, 1712. But then bad weather drove away the Swedish naval escort, while Danish frigates managed to approach and destroy more than 70 Swedish transport ships before their cargo had been unloaded. Now Stenbock stood in Pomerania with an army but with hardly any supplies.

Just to the south were the Saxon and Russian forces that besieged Stralsund, but Stenbock did not want to confront them, and managed to move his army towards the west and Mecklenburg, followed by allied forces. In early November his forces camped just west of Rostock. He managed to agree with the Saxons and Russian for an armistice that would last for a fortnight. That gave him the time he needed to arrange provisions for his army.

But in the meantime Danish forces began to advance towards the east, and on 3 December they reached the town Gadebusch south west of Wismar. With his movements Stenbock had managed to prevent any operational cooperation between his three enemies, but that could soon change. The Russians were too far to the east to reach him, at least in 24 hours, but Saxon cavalry was on its way at a closer range. Stenbock had a window of opportunity of one day and decided to use it.

He advanced closer to the Danish army at Gadebusch and on 9 December 1712 his army of 14,000 Swedes met a Danish force of 16,000 and 3,500 Saxon cavalry. On the battlefield were 30 Swedish guns and 13 Danish. The Danish army was, formally, commanded by the King himself, Frederik IV, but in reality the commander was General Jobst von Scholten, while the Saxons were commanded by Field Marshal Jacob Heinrich von Flemming.

Already at four o'clock in the morning the Danish army began to form its battle positions, and then the men had to wait for several hours in the cold winter weather. First came snow, which at around seven o'clock was transformed to an ice-cold rain that probably lowered the mood among the freezing soldiers.

The Swedish command was of the opinion that the terrain only allowed a frontal attack against the Danish positions, but then the units had to pack themselves between the Radegast stream and a forest area at the village of Wakenstädt. It was now that the Swedish field artillery came to play a decisive role for solving this tactical problem.

Usually the field guns stood more or less still in the battlefield, since movement demanded horses or a lot of manpower. But the Swedish artillery constructor and lieutenant colonel Carl Cronstedt had introduced so called "anmarschbommar" ("marching bars") to the three-pound guns. The bars were long transverse wooden rods through which the gunners could push the guns in front of them, even without any horses. Cronstedt had also introduced so called "fast shots", i.e. ready loads or canisters with grapeshots or bullets. With these canisters well trained gunners could fire 10–14 shots per minute. With the help of the marching bars, and if possible some horses, the artillery could advance 30–40 metres ahead of the infantry, firing 5–7 shots before the foot soldiers reached them, and then if needed repeat the same procedure. The bars allowed the artillery both to advance or retreat if needed. During such a retreat the guns were all the time directed towards the enemy, and could cover the own forces' retreat by firing.

In the Danish–Saxon command there were some disagreements about the best formation. Flemming believed that the Danes had taken a wrong

20. A detail of Swedish soldiers at Gadebusch. Military Archives, Stockholm

position and at a command council Scholten was overruled. The result was a regrouping and confusion when the Danes and Saxons began to change their positions. At that moment the Swedes attacked.

At 11 o'clock the Swedish army moved forward, with the guns in the forefront. After them came infantry in two lines, 600–700 metres broad. Behind them came the rest of the infantry divided into columns, while the cavalry protected the flanks. While the artillery fired upon the enemy, the infantry held its fire until the distance to the enemy was between 12 and 15 steps. An attempt by the Danish cavalry to attack was stopped by combined gun and musket fire from the Swedish frontline. When the infantry had reached the positions of the ahead advancing artillery, the guns were positioned in between the battalion formations, so that a collective fire could be launched.

At the same time the Swedish cavalry on the right wing made a circumvention move, across the Radegast stream, and attacked the Danish left wing. The attack was made with such power that the Danish unit that first was hit, a Hungarian dragoon regiment, was pressed back into the following regiment, and so the congestion and chaos among the Danes grew. The right part of the Swedish infantry then attacked into that part of the battlefield and the pressure upon the Danish units that were squeezed together became even harder. It was not until the Saxon cavalry had arrived that the allied were able to form a new front line.

The left part of the Swedish infantry met the fiercest resistance. The rain and snow had made the powder too wet, while the hands of the men were moist and frozen. In that situation the Swedish infantry attacked with pikes, bayonets and swords, just like at Helsingborg almost three years earlier.

A counterattack from superior Danish and Saxon cavalry (57 squadrons against 28) threatened the Swedish left cavalry wing, but it managed to hold its positions, and also tie down the large enemy cavalry force. This gave the Swedish infantry in the centre the chance to step by step grind down the Danish infantry.

When darkness fell the battle died by itself and the allied forces retreated to the village of Roggendorf, seven kilometres to the west. On the battle field the Swedish army stood still, since Stenbock felt it was meaningless to pursue in the darkness. Left on the battlefield were also the Danish supply carriages and their artillery. During the night of 10 December the Swedish army kept standing (or more likely laying) in battle positions, among thousands of killed and wounded men and horses.

The Danish–Saxon regrouping just before the start of the battle proved to be fatal, and opened a possibility for the Swedes to attack when the enemy was in confusion. But the coordinated and mobile fire from both the artillery and the muskets allowed the Swedish infantry to advance and at the same time more or less fire constantly upon the enemy. The inventions that made the guns mobile were the decisive factor for the outcome of the battle. The Swedish army lost 500 killed and 1,100 wounded, while the Danes lost 2,500 killed and wounded and another 2,500 men were taken prisoners. The Saxons lost 750 killed and wounded and another 100 Saxons became POWs.

Gadebusch lit a hope for the Swedes, but it was the last Swedish victory of the war, and the only one were the field artillery played a decisive role.

Magnus Stenbock, now promoted to field marshal, had won a victory, but the threat from enemies in northern Germany was not averted. He moved the Swedish army to the west into Holstein, before he took quarters in the fortress of Tönningen. There the Swedes were soon surrounded by superior enemies and after a four month long siege Stenbock's army surrendered on 5 May 1713. Together with his men Stenbock went into Danish captivity, and would never be released from it: he died in captivity in 1717.

The Campaign in Tröndelagen, 1718–19

An invasion of Norway would primarily be directed towards Denmark, and its supply of skilled Norwegian sailors and Norwegian shipping timber. But if Sweden managed to neutralise its long western border, that would mean a considerable relief for the defence, and one enemy less to handle. The invasion of 1718 was better planned and prepared, and also larger than the one in 1716. While the main Swedish army under the King's personal command crossed the border in the south and began to build the fortress at Fredriksten, General Carl Gustaf Armfeldt led another army into the Norwegian province Tröndelagen with the goal to reach and conquer Trondheim, the important harbour at the Atlantic coast.

In mid-August 1718 Armfeldt's army of some 10,000 men (of them 5,600 Finns) and 730 mobilised farmers for the handling of the 3,000 horses and the carriages that transported the provisions. Everything the soldiers would eat in Norway had to be taken with them. On narrow roads and along paths

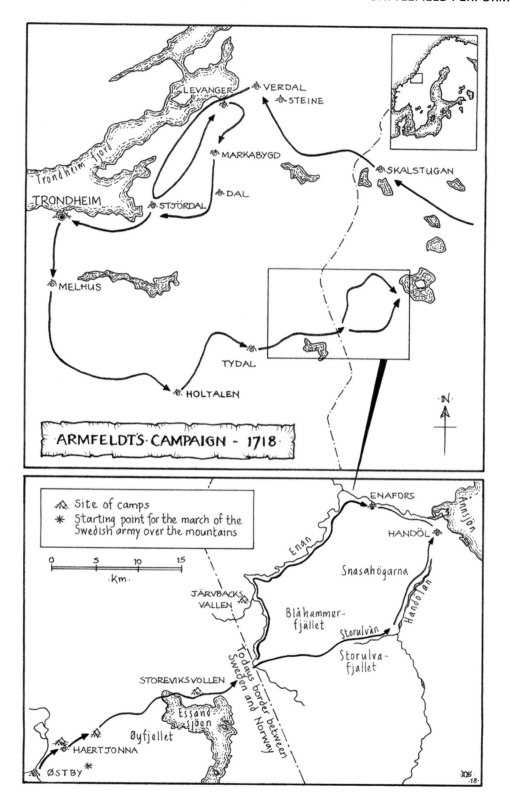

ARMFELDT'S CAMPAIGN - 1718

⚐ Site of camps
✳ Starting point for the march of the
   Swedish army over the mountains

the army marched into Norway and moved about 15 kilometres a day, only disturbed by smaller skirmishes with Norwegian forces.

On 9 October 1718 we can see the first signs that not everything was not in order. The commander of Hälsinge infantry regiment gave an order that all belongings and equipment of dead soldiers should be recorded and still useful shoes and socks should be "given to the men that have not shoes and socks". If there was any garment left over it should be given to "the most naked baggage labourers". These orders were alarming considering the fact that the winter was approaching. The day after, some comfort was given to the men of Hälsinge regiment when schnapps was given to the sick and "tobacco for all".

Some soldiers obviously tried to avoid a march that led them deeper and deeper into enemy territory. Some simply ran away while others "made them sick". Those who tried self-mutilation were beaten by their company commanders' sticks as a first warning.

The Swedish army captured Stene redoubt that was then used as a field hospital, while the army marched further along the River Trondheim towards the town. But now Norwegian forces, often on skies, attacked and killed several Swedish soldiers before disappearing over the mountain slopes, and everyone was warned of possible attacks.

On Saturday 8 November the army reached positions at Väre on the river banks, about 10 kilometres from Trondheim. But the planned assault on the city was postponed and the army marched to a new position at Reningen, south of Trondheim. Here they stayed for a few days, baked bread, slaughtered cattle – the officers were carefully reminded that all skin should be taken care of and used for shoemaking – and took care of the sick. Dysentery spread in the army and numerous soldiers lost all their body strength to diarrhoea, before malnutrition and frostbite contributed to end their lives.

When the news that Charles XII had been killed in southern Norway reached Tröndelagen the northern campaign was also interrupted. There was no military point in trying to conquer Trondheim if the southern army was already marching back to Sweden.

Armfeldt's army marched towards the south and then turned westwards over the border mountains and into Sweden. It was not a very long distance, although difficult terrain. But now it was winter and that was something totally different to a summer march in the mountains. The army started from the last villages in Norway before the border and approached the mountains on New Year's Day 1719, and already after about a day Armfeldt himself and the head of the army reached populated areas in Jämtland on the Swedish side of the border.

But the main part of the army was trapped by a snowstorm while it still was up in the mountains. Between Tydalen in Norway and the small village Handöl in Jämtland at least 3,000 Swedish soldiers succumbed, frozen to death. Most survivors came faltering down the mountain slopes during the 4th and 5th of January, but as late as on the 13th, almost two weeks after the disaster, "people came crawling down to Handöl". The last two survivors, two corporals from Österbotten's regiment in Finland, came down to Handöl as late as 30 January.

The worst time came on the night of 2 January, when officers and men tried to camp in a valley at a mountain lake, still today called "The tarn at the

Swedish camps" ("Svenskelägertjärnarna") on the mountain Öyfjället. When the march was resumed the next morning, hundreds of soldiers had frozen to death during the night. The field priest Nicolaus Idman later told how some of the dead "stood tight to each other as they were living, but when you pushed them a little, the dead fell". On that day discipline dissolved, and now everyone had to save himself. Everything that could burn, even musket stocks and pike staves, were thrown into the fires to give some warmth and at least temporary salvation. But many never came down from the mountains and Jämtland's regiment was hardest hit. Not less than 478 officers and men from that regiment died on the mountains in less than a week around the New Year 1719. In total the campaign cost the province of Jämtland 806 killed, out of a population of about 10,000.

The campaign failed when disease made the army so weak that Armfeldt did not want to risk a costly frontal attack on Trondheim, and after that came the terrible events during the mountain march back to Sweden.

But while the Reaper took a large toll from the Swedish army, he was not gentler in Tröndelagen. In the surrounded Trondheim and in the villages of Tröndelagen, along the march route of the Swedish army more Norwegians died of disease and hunger, and a few of battle wounds, than the number of Swedes that died during their death march over the border mountains. It was a full scale tragedy for both sides, and especially for the population in Jämtland and Tröndelagen.

Södra Stäket, 1719

In the summer of 1719 a Russian archipelago fleet of 132 galleys and 100 smaller, open, boats under the command of General Admiral Fjodor Apraksin, were assembled at Hangö in south-western Finland. The most common galleys were 30 metre long, six metre broad and had a deep of 1.5 metres. Their armament was two main guns and around 10 smaller ones, so-called *nickhakar*. The crews usually consisted of between 150 and 200 men, while the smaller boats had crews of around 50 men. A few of the galleys were larger, among the so-called Cossack galleys that under the ship's deck had room for 20 horses. In total Apraksin had with him 26,000 men.

At nine o'clock in the evening of 10 July the Russian archipelago fleet sat sail and moved out on the Sea of Åland. Then followed some weeks of destruction, fire and violence in the archipelago outside Stockholm. Almost all Swedish forces had been withdrawn from the archipelago in order to defend the capital itself and only at the passage by Vaxholm fortress there was a manned position. The result was that farms, villages and factories were burned down, only churches were spared. Cornfields and wells were destroyed while the cattle was taken away or slaughtered, and iron ores taken from the factories and sunk in the sea. A wave of some 20,000 refugees tried to flee towards Stockholm or the presumed safety of the hinterland. Soon the towns of Södertälje, Trosa, Norrköping, Nyköping, Öregrund, Östhammar and Norrtälje were burning. Together with them seven factories, 20 manors, about 1,000 farms and at least 200 cottages went up in flames.

The big question was, if the Russians also intended to attack Stockholm itself, then how to defend the capital?

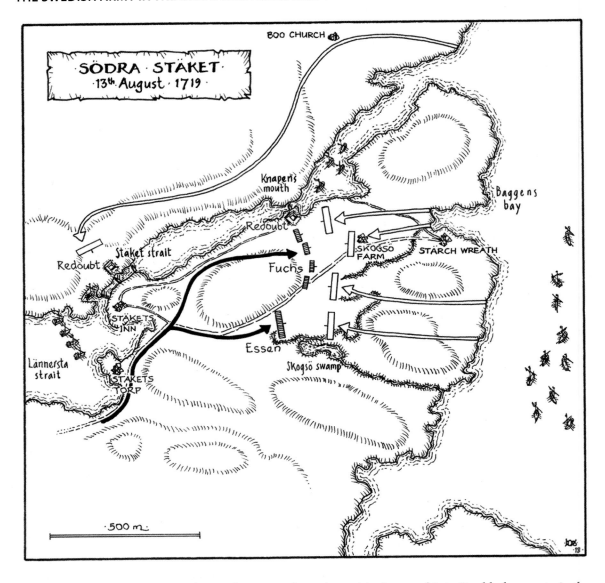

The southern way from the archipelago and into Stockholm went via the narrow Stäket in Nacka, less than 20 kilometres from the city. Colonel Baltzar von Dalheim commanded the effort to block the narrow 1,500 metre long, passage. At its two most narrow spots there was only 30 metres between the beaches. On both places smaller ships filled with stones were sunk into the water, and behind them, in the Lännerstasundet strait, three galleys with guns were positioned. They would be able to fire against an attacker that approached on the other side of those two narrowest spots. Further back was a floating blockhouse, The Black Bear, stationed with 20 heavy guns on board. North of Baggensstäket was a redoubt defended by 400 men infantry and two 3-pound guns. The terrain demanded a combination of land and sea units.

Field Marshal Carl Gustaf Dücker commanded the so-called Stockholm army and he placed units between Stäket and the southern parts of Stockholm. About

10 kilometres away from Baggensstäket stood Dalregementet and Västmanland's Regiments, while Södermanland's Regiment was closer to the expected front.

On 13 August at least 3,000 Russian soldiers, maybe more, arrived on their galleys and landed south of Stäket and advanced past Skogsö manor, where they were met by soldiers from Östgöta-Södermanland's three-männing infantry regiment. Other Russians went ashore north of Stäket and began to move towards the west past Boo church, and began to attack the redoubt north of Stäket, but the Swedish defenders managed to hold their position.

At about seven o'clock in the evening the second battalion of Södermanland's regiment arrived at the scene and reinforced the männing soldiers, who seemed to have stopped the southern Russian columns after Skogsö gård. When it began to get dark the battle subsided. The next day, 14 August, the Russians began to evacuate back to their galleys and rowed away.

The written sources about the battle at Stäket are confusing, and sometimes deliberately untrue, but archaeological excavations have shown that the site of the battle was rather broad and partly in a terrain with small forests and hills, so we can hardly talk about a traditional battlefield. Finds of musket bullets and pieces of hand grenades indicate a fierce battle at some spots, but no traces of supportive gunfire from either side, most likely due to the risk of friendly fire in the growing darkness. The männing regiments from Östergötland and Södermanland obviously managed to halt, or at least slow down, the Russian advance, until one of the battalions from Södermanland's infantry regiment arrived and made the Russians retreat and sail, or rather row, away.

Stockholm was saved, but the devastation in the archipelago continued for some days. However at the last minute Swedish cavalry from the Life Dragoons managed to prevent landed Russian troops advancing and destroying Vira Bruk north of Stockholm, the main manufacturer of swords for the army, but five days after the battle the Russian galleys regrouped and began to go back towards the east, across Åland's Sea. After seven hours of rowing they reached Ledsund on Åland.

Rather soon after the Russian retreat people began to return to the archipelago, and tried to rebuild their burned homes and see what could be saved from their destroyed lands. The government gave most of them tax exemption for four years to support the reconstruction of the archipelago.

There has been a lot of criticism about the decision, ultimately by Prince Fredrik I and Field Marshal Dücker, to concentrate almost all the defensive effort on Stockholm and leave the archipelago more or less defenceless. But the alternative would have resulted in a weakness along the whole defence line. Now the Swedish command tried to achieve local superiority where it was most important, at the capital. This was without any doubt the most effective way to meet a very mobile enemy that could strike fast in different directions. There were very few Swedish naval units that could operate in these shallow waters; the sailing navy could not, and was also most needed in the southern parts of the Baltic Sea as a guard against the Danish navy.

There is no question of the extent of the disaster that hit the archipelago and several small coastal towns, but from a military point of view the Swedish command probably made the best of an impossible situation.

9

Connections Between Two Parallel Wars

The Great Northern War of course dominated the daily life of the Swedish military during the first two decades of the 18th century. But while it was being fought in northern and eastern Europe, the western and southern parts of Europe as well as North America were ravaged by the Spanish War of Succession. This large conflict between on the one hand France allied with Spain and Savoy (who changed side in 1703), and on the other Great Britain, the Netherlands, the Emperor in Vienna as well as several German states, especially Bavaria, lasted between 1701 and 1713–1714.

While a British diplomat, James Jefferyes, followed the Swedish army on its way deeper and deeper into Russia during the years 1707–09, there was no corresponding Swedish observer in the large war in the west. That did not mean that Sweden lacked interest in the West European war, far from it. For Sweden it was essential that her traditional ally, France, did not suffer a defeat. But at the same time it was essential to balance the British naval and commercial interests in the Baltic region, especially when Swedish privateers attacked British ships sailing for Russian-controlled ports. On one hand an open war with Great Britain was not allowed to break out, on the other it was essential for Sweden to convince London to prevent a far too strong Russian dominance in the Baltic region. This activity towards Paris, Den Haag and London was an almost impossible task for the Swedish diplomacy.

But the Swedish military had a special interest for the War of the Spanish Succession. In particular the army collected and studied numerous battle plans and sieges in order to follow operational and tactical development in the west. Such collecting of plans had been done since the Thirty Years' War, but the activity expanded enormously during the Spanish War of Succession.

Today there are still extant 469 maps and plans showing military events during the years 1701–13, all of them preserved at the Military Archives (Krigsarkivet) in Stockholm, and they represent a minimum figure of how much was once collected by Swedish intelligence. If we take one year, 1703, as an example, there are 70 plans preserved, gathered by the Swedish fortification section, which handled these kinds of intelligence operations. They represent a large number of places, from the southern Netherlands to southern Germany and Tyrol, to northern Italy:

Battle plans from the year 1703 in Western Europe, collected by the Swedish Kept at the Military Archives, Stockholm, in the collection *Utländska krigsplaner* (*Foreign battle plans*) volume XII: 27 ½ a, 27 ½ c-53 b.			
Mantua (1701–03)	3	Breisach	2
Rheinberg	1	Schwenningen and Hochstedt	5
The Stolhofen Line	4	Hausheim	2
Baden	1	Limburg	3
The Netherlands	2	Saar	1
Maastricht	3	Landau (Rheinland Pfalz)	1
Bonn	8	Geldern	3
Stecken	1	Augsburg	5
Kufstein	1	Wasseiges & Jandrain	4
Eckeren	6	Rothenberg	3
Dillingen & Laningen	5	Vilshofen	1
Huy	3	San Salvador (Brazil)	2

We do not know exactly when these plans were collected. Some are obviously documents of propaganda, produced by the winner, but most of them can be described as relics of the military planning and operational process. Most certainly they were collected during or immediately after the war. With this collection of maps and plans the Swedish army formed a rather good picture of important parts of the Spanish War of Succession. The collection could be used, not only by those who wanted to follow the events during the war in the west, but also for educating younger officers in operational and tactical problems.

Sometimes the Swedes also managed to get their hands on other intelligence material. In that same year, 1703, a thick report was written in Cologne about France – its court, financial administration and military capacity – by "Eines Hohen Ministri" ("A High Minister"). We do not know who that man was, but obviously he had good insights into the France of Louis XIV, and a copy of the report landed in Sweden. Here high-ranking Swedish officers could read a very insightful description of Europe's largest army, some 200,000 strong. The anonymous writer gave information about a number of high-ranking French officers and their titles as well as their professional skill.

Several Swedish officers also participated in the Spanish War of Succession. Most of them belonged to the French regiment Royal Suédois, which between 1690 and 1791 functioned as a kind of educational unit for several hundred Swedish officers. Some of them participated in the campaigns of the French army, for instance the battle of Nijmegen, the siege of Hulst and the conquests of Roermond and Andernach in 1702. During 1703 the Royal Suédois was one of the regiments that took part in the French conquest of Eckeren, and the following year the regiment was a part of the French army that operated along the Mosel in western Germany.

The commander of the regiment at this time was Colonel (from 1705 Major General) Erik Sparre. During the years he commanded the Royal

Suédois between 30 and 40 Swedish officers served with the regiment, which corresponds to about the half of its entire officer corps. After the battle of Eckeren in 1703 Sparre requested dismissal and joined Charles XII and the Swedish army in Poland. Here he commanded a Pomeranian regiment during the siege of Thorn, and participated in the conquest of that town, before he left Poland in November the same year and returned to his French regiment.

Under other commanders the Royal Suédois participated in the battles of Ramilles, Oudenaarde and Malplaquet as well as the conquest of Freiburg. This was an important way for the Swedish army to get experience from and information about the Spanish War of Succession. Most likely some of the still existing maps and plans came to Sweden via some of these officers.

The most distinguished Swedish (to be) officer that participated in the war in the west was Friedrich of Hessen-Kassel (1676–1751). As the heir to the Land Grafschaft Hessen-Kassel Friedrich first became commander of an infantry regiment and then a dragoon regiment in Hessen, before in 1696 serving in the Netherlands army and later in the Prussian army. The main part of his career took place during the Spanish War of Succession. Friedrich himself later said that he had two military teachers, the Hessian General Spiegel and Eugène of Savoy. Friedrich became a qualified officer and commanded Hessian units in a march across the Alps in the summer of 1706 and at Toulon in 1707. At Malplaquet he commanded a decisive cavalry charge.

In 1715 Friedrich married Ulrika Eleonora, Charles XII's sister, and the same year he was appointed commander of the Swedish units that were detached to defend Stockholm and the eastern coast. During the terrible summer of 1719 he managed to save Stockholm from the Russians, although at the cost of a devastated archipelago. When Charles XII was killed in 1718 Ulrika Eleonora was elected Queen in early 1719, but already in 1720 Friedrich was elected as King Fredrik I, and as such he would rule for three decades.

King Fredrik I has very often been described as a frivolous, if not lazy and uninterested King. But that judgement is rather unfair, since he was one of the most experienced monarchs Sweden had had, although most of his military career took place before he came to Sweden. It is tempting to guess that many of the maps and battle plans from the Spanish War of Succession still kept in Sweden arrived with Fredrik, when he on New Year's Eve 1714 he arrived at Karlshamn and Sweden; although that remains only a guess.

Besides the Swedish officers who served in the war in the west, and the intelligence gathering of maps and plans, Sweden also recruited mercenaries among veterans from the Spanish War of Succession. In 1714, when that war had ended with the peace treaties in Utrecht in 1713 and Rastatt in 1714, one dragoon regiment and one infantry regiment (both German) were recruited. They had been in the service of Great Britain and the Netherlands before they joined the Swedish army. Another German infantry regiment in allied service in 1712 came to surrender to a Swedish force and passed to Swedish service.

To summarise: we can see a number of different connections between the Swedish army and the Spanish War of Succession, both in officers with experience from both sides in that conflict, as well as the use of veteran units from the allied armies. But also important is the large number of battle plans and maps from the war in the west, indicating ambitious intelligence work from the Swedish military. Exactly how the experience from and knowledge about operations and tactical behaviour during the Spanish succession war was used in Sweden we will never be able to tell, only that an active interest and much knowledge was there.

10

Conclusions

The Carolean army that went to war in 1700 used to be regarded as perhaps the best trained that Sweden ever mustered. That army also managed to resist its enemies for nine years before it met its fate at Poltava in the summer of 1709. But after that the war continued for another 12 years. The explanation for that is partly that Sweden managed to rebuild her army, not once but twice and even a third time. That demonstrates the fundamental efficiency of the military organisation.

But at the same time it is important to stress the lack of coordination between Sweden's three main enemies, Russia, Denmark and Saxony-Poland. This was a fundamental presumption for the Swedish successes. Time after time the Swedes managed to confront and defeat one enemy at the time, instead of having to meet a united and overwhelming power. When her enemies sometimes managed to carry out relatively coordinated operations, such as in northern Germany during the years 1713–16, their superiority became to large for the Swedes to handle.

Another Swedish advantage was that the Russian successes rather soon led to growing dissatisfaction and suspicion, first among the Poles and Saxons, then by the Danes and later also in Hannover and Great Britain. This meant that the coalition could not take full advantage of the Swedish defeats against the Russians.

All three main enemies went to war in 1700 to regain lost territories. Denmark finally failed to recapture Scania and other provinces east of Öresund with the defeat at Helsingborg in 1710. Even though the dream of revenge lived for another century among many leading Danes, the events of 1709–10 were the last serious attempt to recapture the lost territories.

For Poland-Saxony, attempts to reconquer lost Polish territories in Livonia and Estonia totally failed. Instead both Poland, but also to some extent Saxony, were devastated during years of war against the Swedes. It finally was Russia that ended up as the big winner, and the Russian advance towards the Baltic Sea coast is of course symbolised by the foundation of the new city of St Petersburg in 1703. Without any exaggeration one can say that the result of the Great Northern War was, besides the collapse of the Swedish empire, the rise of Russia as a great power, and at the same time the first step on the road towards the coming Polish disaster, the partition of Poland in the late 18th century. The war also resulted in Sweden's loss of Stettin and the eastern part of Swedish Pomerania to Prussia, one important step on Prussia's road to being the most important power in Germany, stronger than Saxony and later also Austria.

Besides the lack of cooperation between the enemies, how could it be that Sweden managed to resist for another 12 years after Poltava? First of all, after the loss of her Baltic provinces, Sweden's fighting capability was stiffened. The organisation of a new army was not finished soon enough to save Estonia, Latvia and Ingria, but in time to save Scania.

The Carolean army's fundamental tactical and operational efficiency time after time resulted in victories against superior, but poorly-led and coordinated enemies. In her doctrine the Swedish army was not more offensive in her tactical behaviour than her enemies, but due to better leadership and training the Swedish units were able to conduct more offensive tactics than her enemies.

Important actions were also made by the Swedish navy, which from the outbreak of the war in 1700 dominated the Baltic Sea for the first half of the war, and thus secured the lines of sea communication between Sweden proper and the field armies on the other side. It was during the middle and later parts of the 1710s that the naval defence began to fail due to pressure from the Danish and the growing Russian sailing fleets, as well as the Russian archipelago fleet. Here we have a good part of, although not the whole, explanation as to why Sweden collapsed in 1721 and not in 1709.

However, from a strategic point of view Sweden had serious problems, especially when King Charles XII between 1709 and 1714 was in exile in Ottoman Turkey. The government (*riksrådet* – the riksrad) back in Stockholm tried to gain the King's permission to give up all Swedish possessions in Germany, and especially Pomerania, as a way to end the wars against Prussia and Hannover. But Charles XII refused to give an inch of Swedish soil. Everyone, the King and the government, agreed that Russia was the main enemy, and the most dangerous one. But how to defeat the Russians and to reconquer lost territories, that they could not agree upon.

When the King died in November 1718 most of the strength of Sweden had run out. No new offensive operations were carried out, and at the negotiating table peace treaties were signed with Hannover in 1719, and Prussia and Denmark in 1720. Besides that, a treaty of financial and naval support for the war against Russia was signed with Great Britain, also in 1720.

But Sweden could not manage to continue an offensive war against Russia on her own. There were plans to get assistance of Prussian troops to retake Estonia, maybe also Livonia. But nothing came out of these plans. In peace negotiations with Russia Sweden tried, as long as possible, to keep the city of Reval. If that had succeeded the Swedes would have had positions on both sides of the Gulf of Finland, but also that failed. But important enough was that the larger part of Finland was given back to Sweden by the Russians in the peace treaty of 1721, although the most south-eastern part of Finland, as well as Ingria, Estonia and Livonia, were lost.

After the peace in 1721 the Carolean army was rebuilt, with the same regular units and the same proportions between infantry, cavalry and dragoons as in 1700. The allotment system was kept as the main way to recruit and finance officers and men, although completed with some enlisted units. It was thought that the reason for the defeat in the war was not any failures within or by the army, but simply that Sweden had too many enemies.

During the 1720s it was very clear that Sweden had tried to rebuild the army of 1699 or of 1700, but success was limited. Too many officers and soldiers had been killed during the 21 years of war, and the financial resources directed to the armed forces were more limited than they had been at the end of the 17th century. Despite more than two decades of peace after 1721, the army was not given the same opportunity for regular training and larger exercises than it had during the 1680s and 1690s. So, during the next war against Russia in 1741–43 it became clear that the Swedish army could not measure up.

The Carolean army, with its combination of quality and quantity, did not survive the Great Northern War, despite later ambitions and dreams for its revival.

Appendix

List of Army Units, 1700-21

Please note that several of the units mentioned (especially the regular ones) here were raised in the years 1700–01 and then lost at Poltava in June, 1709, but later once again raised one or a few years after that battle. Some units were then again lost at the surrender of Tönningen 1713, and once again, for a third time, raised. In their second and third incarnation they often included remains of one or several temporary regiments. During the raise of new units in 1710, after Poltava, several temporary units were merged into the new regular ones.

Many of the regular regiments were recruited in the different provinces or counties, such as Uppland in central Sweden or Björneborg in Finland.

Regular Infantry
1. Lifeguard of Foot
2. Uppland's regiment
3. Skaraborg's regiment
4. Södermanland's regiment
5. Kronoberg's regiment
6. Jönköping's regiment
7. Kalmar regiment
8. Dalarna's regiment (Dalecarlia regiment)
9. Östgöta regiment
10. Hälsinge regiment
11. Älvsborg's regiment
12. Västgöta-Dal's regiment
13. Västmanland's regiment
14. Västerbotten's regiment
15. Jämtland's regement (see also Jämtland's dragoon regiment below)
16. Närke-Värmland's regiment
17. Björneborg county's infantry regiment
18. Nyland's infantry regiment
19. Savolax and Nyslott counties infantry regiment
20. Tavastehus läns infantry regiment
21. Viborg county's (Villmanstrand's) infantry regiment

22.   Åbo län's infantry regiment
23.   Österbotten's infantry regiment
24.   King's Own Swedish Life Regiment of Foot, –1716/1719
25.   Queen's Own Life Regiment of Foot, –1715
26.   Quartermaster's Company (Enspännarkompaniet; used for planning and preparation of the army's campsites).
27.   The Grenadier Battalion. Organised in early 1717 by 56 officers and 512 soldiers, selected from eight different regular and temporary allotted regiments. It worked like an elite unit, mainly for the defence of Gothenburg. Dissolved in 1719 and the remains included in the Lifeguard.

Regular Cavalry

1.   The Lifeguard Corps (*Livdrabantkåren*; an exclusive unit serving as the King's personal lifeguard)
2.   The Nobility Banner (*Adelsfanan*; recruited among the nobility and their servants)
3.   Life Regiment of Horse
4.   Småland's cavalry regiment
5.   Västgöta cavalry regiment
6.   Östgöta cavalry regiment
7.   Jämtland's cavalry company
8.   Queen Mother's (*Riksänkedrottningens*) Life Regiment of Horse
9.   Northern Scanian (*Norra Skånska*) cavalry regiment
10.   Southern Scanian (*Södra Skånska*) cavalry regiment
11.   Viborg county cavalry regiment
12.   Nyland and Tavastehus counties' cavalry regiment
13.   Åbo and Björneborg counties' cavalry regiment
14.   Finnish enlisted battalion, 1711–19

Regular Dragoons

1.   Bohuslän's dragoon squadron
2.   Jämtland's dragoon regiment. In 1700 ⅓ of the regiment was mounted and the rest, besides the cavalry company (see above) were infantry.
3.   Carelian dragoon squadron/Finnish dragoons/Carelian regular dragoon regiment
4.   The Life Dragoon regiment. Formed in 1721 from the remains of three other regiments.
5.   Bender's dragoon regiment, 1712–16

Temporary Regiments

Männing regiment: in the allotment system a group of farmers (a "rote" of mostly 3–10 farms depending of their size) raised one infantry soldier in an ordinary infantry regiment of 1,200 men, or a more wealthy farmer raised one soldier with a horse for a cavalry regiment of 1,000 men. After the outbreak of the war three "rotar" or three wealthier farmers raised a three-männing (three men) regiment. The original military burdon was broadened with one third, and then with four- and five-männing regiments based on the same principle.

Three-, Four- and Five-männing Regiments of Horse
1. Upplands (the Life Regiment) and Östgöta three-männing regiment 1700–09, 1712–19
2. Västgöta three- and five-männing regiment 1700–21
3. Scania's three- and four-männing regiment 1700–21
4. Åbo, Nyland's and Viborg's counties three-männing regiment 1700–01
5. Uppland's (and other counties) five-männing regiment 1703–21

Three-, Four- and Five-männing Regiments of Foot
1. Uppland's (Västmanland's and Dalarnas') three-männing regiment 1700–09, 1712–19
2. Östgöta (and Södermanland's) three-männing regiment 1700–03, 1712–21
3. Småland's three-männing regiment 1700–09, 1712–19
4. Västgöta three-männing regiment 1700–19. In 1719 converted to the Garrison Regiment in Gothenburg, and retracted in 1801
5. Närke and Värmland's three-männing regiment 1700–09, 1712–20
6. Åbo, Björneborg's and Nyland's three-männing regiment 1700–09
7. Tavastehus', Viborgs' and Savolax' three-männing regiment 1700–04
8. Hälsinge, Gästrike and Western Norrland's (Västernorrlands) three- and five-männing regiment 1700–19
9. Uppland's, Södermanland's, Västmanland's and Dalarnas' five-männing regiment 1703–20. In 1720 this regiment formed one of the garrison regiments in Stralsund, Pomerania
10. Västgöta, Närke's and Värmland's five-männing regiment 1703–20. In 1720 this regiment formed one of the garrison regiments in Stralsund, Pomerania
11. Småland's and Östergötland's five-männing regiment 1703–19
12. Småland's three- and five-männing regiment 1719–21. Formed by no. 3 and 11 above. From 1721 it became a garrison regiment in Scania (Skåne).

Reduplication and Conscription Regiments of Foot (*Fördubblings- och utskrivningsregementen till häst*)
1. Åbo county's reduplication regiment (*Åbo läns fördubblingsregemente*) 1701–10
2. Nyland county's reduplication regiment (*Nylands läns fördubblingsregemente*) 1701–10
3. Viborg county's reduplication regiment (*Viborgs läns fördubblingsregemente*) 1701–10

Reduplication and Conscription Units of Foot (*Fördubblings- och utskrivningsförband till fot*)
1. Åbo county's reduplication battalion 1701-10

2.   Björneborg county's reduplication battalion 1701–10
3.   Tavastehus county's reduplication battalion 1701–10
4.   Nyland county's reduplication battalion 1701–10
5.   Viborg county's reduplication battalion 1701–10
6.   Savolax reduplication battalion 1701–10
7.   Eastern Scanian conscription regiment 1711–22. In 1722 merged into a garrison regiment in Malmö
8.   Western Scanian conscription regiment 1711–22. In 1722 merged into a garrison regiment in Malmö
9.   Halland's conscription regiment 1711–21

Estate Dragoons (*Ståndsdragoner*)

These units were set up by wealthier groups in society, such as the nobility, the clergy, owners of some factories, civil servants etc. The Swedish word "*stånd*" ("estate") refers to social groups (including the farmers) but is here used for higher social stratas in society.

1.   Uppland's estate dragoon regiment 1700–09, 1712–21
2.   Scanian estate dragoon regiment 1700–09, 1712–21
3.   Västgöta estate dragoon regiment 1703–17
4.   Finnish estate dragoon battalion 1700–07
5.   Gotland's estate dragoon company 1700–21
6.   Österbotten's estate dragoon company, raised 1700–01

Mining Units (*Bergsförband*)

The Swedish word refers to areas and groups with the mining as well as the copper and iron ore industry. Theses areas were exempted from military service of any kind, but during the war of 1700–21 they also had to contribute to the military effort with units of their own.

1.   Mining battalion Sinclair 1701–05
2.   Mining battalion Zeedt 1703–05
3.   The 'new' mining regiment, 1705–22. Formed when the above battalions of Zeedt and Sinclair merged. In 1722 the regiment was transformed to a garrison regiment in Malmö

German Regiments

A large number of regiments and other units were recruited in Sweden's German provinces (Pomerania, Wismar, Bremen-Verden), both before and during the war. A large proportion of the army's dragoon units came from Germany. Several of these units were lost at Poltava in 1709, but the main part disappeared in connection with the surrenders of Stralsund in 1715 and Wismar in 1716.

Infantry

1.   King's Own German Life Regiment of Foot, –1715
2.   Wismar's governors' regiment, –1716
3.   Stralsund's infantry regiment, –1715
4.   Queen Mothers (*Riksänkedrottningens*) Life Regiment of Foot, –1715

5.   Stade's garrison regiment, –1715
6.   Wismar's garrison regiment, –1715
7.   Bremen's infantry regiment, –1715
8.   Pomeranian infantry regiment, –1715
9.   Elbing's infantry regiment 1703–15
10. Bremen's rural militia regiment (*lantregemente*) 1710–12
11. Stettin's rural militia regiment (infantry regiment) 1710–15
12. Anklam's rural militia regiment (infantry regiment) 1710–15
13. Rügen's rural militia- or marine regiment 1710–15

Cavalry
1.   Bremen's cavalry regiment 1700–15
2.   Pomerania's cavalry regiment 1698–1715
3.   Holstein's cavalry regiment 1714–15
4.   The Nobility Banner in Pomerania
5.   The Nobility Banner in Bremen-Verden

Dragoons
1)   Bremen's dragoon regiment 1699–1715
2)   Verden's dragoon regiment 1702–15
3)   Pomerania's dragoon regiment 1703–15
4)   Dücker's dragoon regiment/Prussian dragoon regiment 1703–09
5)   Taube's dragoon regiment/Schlesian dragoon regiment 1703–09
6)   Stenbock's dragoon regiment 1703–09 (from 1706: Hielm's regiment)
7)   Meyerfelt's dragoon regiment 1703–09
8)   Goertz' dragoon regiment 1706–09 (from 1707: Albedyll's regiment)
9)   Gyllenstierna's dragoon regiment 1707–09
10) Schwerin's dragoon regiment 1710–12
11) Wismar's (Bassewitz') dragoon regiment 1711–15
12) Barth's dragoon regiment 1714–15 (Vietinghof 1714–15, Düring 1715)
13) Wismar's cavalry corps 1713–14
14) Holstein's dragoon guard (Dernaths) 1714–15. This unit had since 1703 participated in the Spanish War of Succession, and had been paid for by Great Britain and the Netherlands. After its surrender in Stralsund in 1715 the officers and men were put into several Danish and Prussian units.
15) German dragoon regiment 1715–1721 (Tettenborn 1715–17, Düring 1717–21)

Units in the Baltic Provinces of Ingria, Estonia and Livonia
The allotment system was never introduced in Sweden's Baltic provinces. instead soldiers were recruited by enlistment and conscription. Many of the units were of the militia type with relatively low quality. Many units were also smaller than regimental size. During the first years of the war there were five Estonian and 14 Livonian militia battalions. Many of the Livonian units surrendered in Riga in 1710.

During the Swedish Era (1561–1710/1721) Estonia corresponded to the northern half of today's Estonia, while Livonia corresponded to todays southern Estonia and northern Latvia (including Riga, and with the River Düna (Daugava) as the southern border. Ingria was, and is, the province from Narva in the west to Ladoga in the east. In its most northern part, along the River Neva, the Russian city of St Petersburg was founded in 1703, on the ruins of an older Swedish city, Nyen.

Infantry
1. The Governor's regiment in Riga, –1710
2. The garrison regiment in Riga, –1710
3. A Livonian infantry regiment, –1710
4. A Livonian infantry regiment 1700/01–1710
5. A Livonian infantry regiment 1703–10
6. A Livonian infantry regiment 1703–10. Pernau garrison regiment
7. A Livonian infantry regiment 1704–1710
8. The garrison regiment in Narva, –1704
9. The Estonian infantry regiment 1700–09
10. The Estonian infantry regiment 1702–10
11. The Ingrian (*Ingermanländska*) infantry regiment 1700–10
12. A Livonian infantry battalion 1700–10. Wiped out at Lesnaja in 1708 and Poltava in 1709
13. A Livonian infantry battalion 1700–10. The remnants surrendered at Reval (Tallinn) in 1710
14. A Livonian infantry battalion 1700–04. Surrendered in Dorpat (Tartu)
15. A Livonian infantry battalion 1703–04. Surrendered in Dorpat
16. The militia regiment (*lantmilisregemente*) of Jerwen's region 1701–04. Surrendered at Narva in 1704
17. The militia regiment of Wieren's region 1701–04. Surrendered at Narva in 1704
18. The (second) militia regiment of Wieren's region 1701–04 Surrendered at Narva in 1704
19. The militia regiment of Harrien region 1701–10. Surrendered at Reval in 1710
20) The battalion of the city mayor (*stadsmajoren*) of Reval 1707–10
21) Lewenhaupt's free company. Recruited in Livonia, fought in Livonia and Curia (Kurland), mentioned 1704

Cavalry
1. The Nobility Banner in Estonia and Ingria
2. The Nobility Nanner in Livonia and on the island of Ösel (Saaremaa)
3. The reduplication of the Estonian Nobility Banner 1700–10
4. The reduplication of the Livonian Nobility Banner 1700–09
5. Queens Own Life Regiment of Horse/Estonian cavalry regiment

Dragoons
1. The Estonian estate dragoon battalion 1701–10

2) The Livonian estate dragoon battalion 1700–10
3) The dragoon battalion of Ösel 1700–09
4) The estate dragoons of Ingria. Organised in 1700 in Ingria and the county of Kexholm (eastern Finland)
5) The Ingrian dragoon regiment 1700–19
6) The Livonian dragoon regiment 1700–03
7) The Livonian dragoon regiment (Schlippenbach's) 1700–09. After Poltava some of the men went into Russian service
8) Livonian dragoon squadron 1701–09(?)
9) Livonian dragoon squadron 1700–10. Surrendered at Riga.
10) The militia dragoon squadron of Ösel 1700–08.
11) The militia dragoon squadron of Estonia 1700–01
12) Laurentzen's free dragoons 1701–06. Organised by the burghers in the cities of Venden (Cesis), Wolmar (Valmiera), Walk (Valga) and Lemsal (Limbazi)

Polish Units

1. The Gelding (Vallack) or Volloscher regiment 1706–15. Formed by Polish and Lithuanian free companies. From 1709 (at Bender) called Niester's dragoon regiment
2. The Polish Regiment of Horse 1715–18. Formed by Polish soldiers from the above
3. Smiegelski's Polish Dragoon Corps. Organised as a free corps in Poland and surrendered at Tönningen in 1713

Units Organised by POWs

1. Goertz' Infantry Regiment. Organised from Saxon POWs after Fraustadt in 1706 and wiped out at Kalisch in the same year
2. The Swiss Battalion. Organized with French and Swiss soldiers in Saxon service becoming POWs at Fraustadt in 1706. Wiped out at Kalisch in the same year
3. The French Battalion. Organised with French in Saxon service after Fraustadt in 1706, and wiped out at Kalisch the same year
4. The French Dragoon Regiment. Recruited among French soldiers in Poland in 1707, dissolved after an attempt to retreat towards Pomerania in 1709. A handful of men followed Charles XII to Demotika in Turkey (today in north-eastern Greece) where they joined Niester's Dragoon Regiment (see Polish units above).
5. The Bavarian Infantry Regiment. Organised with Swiss in Saxon service after Fraustadt in 1706, and wiped out at Kalisch the same year
6. The Foreign Regiment (*Främlingsregementet*) 1706–10. Consisted of mostly Germans (not Saxons), French and Swiss. Dissolved after mass desertions
7. The Saxon Infantry Regiment 1707–21. Organised with Saxon POWs after Fraustadt in 1706
8. The Saxon Infantry Battalion (Straelborn) 1707–10. Organised with Saxon POWs after Fraustadt in 1706

9.   The Saxon Infantry Battalion (Boye). Organised with Saxon POWs after Fraustadt in 1706

10.   The Saxon Infantry Battalion (Seulenberg) 1707–09. Organised with Saxon POWs after Fraustadt in 1706. Wiped out at Konkanpää, Ingria, 1708

11.   The German Infantry Battalion (Stöhr) 1710–14. Organised with Danish and German POWs after Helsingborg in 1710

12.   The Infantry Regiment of the Rhein (Leutrum) 1712–15. This was paid for by the British during the Spanish War of Succession when it in 1712 surrendered to Swedish forces in Zweibrücken. Then it went into Swedish service, but after the surrender of Stralsund the officers and men were put into several Danish and Prussian units

13)   The infantry regiment of Holstein 1714–15. This regiment had since 1703 participated in the Spanish War of Succession in the service of Great Britain and the Netherlands

14)   The Battalion of Zweibrücken 1714–19

Besides all the units listed above the burghers in several cities were obliged to make service in their own cities' military corps. In the capital Stockholm, by far the largest city, there was one military corps of foot and one of horse. These units were to defend their home town but never be sent outside it.

In some parts of the country, mainly Scania in the south, Vestrogothia, Dalsland and Värmland in the south-west and parts of Finland armed arrays of farmers were organised when the regular army units in the region were too weak. But it was only in Finland that these arrays were sent into battle, especially at Storkyro in 1714. In Finland there were also so-called free companies organised under professional military command. They carried on a kind of guerrilla war against the Russian army that in 1713–14 conquered Finland. Several of these companies carried out important operations behind the Russian lines, while others degenerated into plain robbers that tormented their own civilian population.

Colour Plate Commentaries

Artwork, research and captions by Sergey Shamenkov

Translation by Boris Megorsky

Plate 1: General, staff officer, and Charles XII

General in a double-breasted coat. This cut is represented on a number of period portraits of Swedish officers and generals. The loops of such coats could be laid with lace, buttons could be as usual brass and gold-plated, or covered with lace as in the picture. The general is wearing a cuirass over the leather vest. The hat has no lace in imitation of the old fashion, and the fashion for the simplicity of the very King Charles XII. The sword belt is decorated with zigzags embossed on the skin.

Staff officer. The officer has a simple everyday officer's uniform. Many portraits of senior officers and generals show such simple uniforms, without decoration. The coat is all blue. The sword belt has a buckle and hook for a carbine. The coat is blue, with the same lining, waistcoat and trousers. The gorget bears the King's cipher after the piece from the Artillery Museum in St Petersburg. Unlike the King, who has plain elkskin sword belt, this officer wears a belt embroidered with silver thread.

Charles XII in the year 1700. The King is wearing a warm fur-lined coat. This type of coat is depicted on many period portraits of the King, and is also depicted on the portraits of Swedish officers and commanders of the late 17th and early 18th centuries.

Plate 2: Private of Life Dragoons, Trooper of Life Regiment, Corporal Drabant

This private of the Life (*Leib, Liv*) Dragoons has uniform and equipment as the trooper (centre), only with brass buttons.

Trooper of Life Regiment, 1707. Hat with gold lace, blue coat with blue lining, pewter buttons, leather waistcoat and trousers. Equipment consists of a sword with a sheath on a leather sword belt with brass buckle and an elkskin shoulder belt with hook and carbine.

Corporal Drabant. His hat is trimmed with gold lace, on the left side there is a bundle of straw as a cockade. The blue coat is lined light blue, laid along breast and loops with gold lace; the vest has lace also. Buttons are gilded. Lace also decorated belts. The drabants wore cuirasses, but a few years after the outbreak of the war, these were abandoned.

Plate 3: 'Elite infantry': Guards Regiment Lifeguard officer, pikeman and musketeer

Officer (lieutenant) of the Guards infantry regiment, 1700. The hat and the officer's entire uniform are trimmed with gold lace. The uniform is blue with a light blue lining, with gilded buttons. The sword belt is also trimmed with gold lace, the buckle is gilded. Arms: a half-pike and sword.

Pikeman (private) of the Guards infantry regiment, 1700. The uniform is identical to the officer, except the loopholes are laid out with yellow cloth. The cloak is blue with a yellow lining and a yellow collar, fastened at the front of the collar with metal buckles. Straw is inserted in the boots for insulation. Armed with pike and sword.

The musketeer, a private of the Guards infantry regiment, displays a pose of "present arms" 1700–1709. His hat is trimmed with lace: in 1700 silk lace of a mixture of gold and silver threads, but in 1709 just white threads. The coat is blue with yellow lining; buttons tin; camisoles and pants yellow elk skin; knitted woollen yellow stockings, with leather garters under the knee; leather shoes with buckles of yellow metal. Equipment consists of an elk skin sword belt, a buckle of yellow metal, the same band for a cartridge bag. The lid of the black leather cartridge box is covered with a blue cloth with a cloth appliqué in the form of a royal monogram. At the end of the war in 1716–1718, to the crown and monogram were added laurel branches and small crowns in the corners of the bag. The powder horn/primer is suspended on the sword belt. The armament consists of a musket, bayonet and a sword.

Plate 4: 'Elite infantry': Grenadier, close-up details of equipment and various styles of grenadier's cap (not worn on campaign)

Grenadier (top) of B. Mellin's regiment (*Estländskt infanterieregemente*) 1700. The grenadier is depicted at the moment before the attack. Coat blue with yellow lining, camisole elk, breeches and stockings blue. Grenadier's cap of blue cloth with a standing front flap of yellow cloth; on the flap there are five sewn grenades. In front of the cap there is a cipher CXII, sewn from yellow cloth, with the same two sides of lions holding a crown of yellow cloth over the cipher. On the back, the inscription GRENADIERS DU COMTE MELIN, above the inscription is the crown, and below that two palm branches cross-laid. At the top is a yellow woollen tassel. Grenadiers were armed like musketeers: a musket with a flintlock, bayonet and sword. The grenadier's musket of the grenadier had a shoulder sling. The sword and bayonet were worn on the sword belt. The cartridge bag for grenadiers was the same model as that of the musketeer; a brass match case was attached to the belt on the front. On the cover of the cartridge bag, sewn applique in the form of a royal monogram with a crown, leather. The leather grenade bag in this case is yellow. The lid of the grenade bag could also be decorated with a leather appliqué in the form of a royal monogram. A grenade bag was worn over the right shoulder. Most likely grenade bags, with grenades, were not worn all the time, but issued as needed before the battle. During the battle the grenadiers reformed and occupied positions in the centre in front of the banner group. According to the Swedish infantry regulations of 1701, during the battle 8 grenadiers stood out for the protection of the captain.

Grenadier (left) from a Saxon recruited regiment (*Sachsiska infanteriregementet*) 1717. The grenadier stands in position before throwing a grenade. The uniform is of the same type as previously described, coat and breeches made of blue cloth. The equipment and weapons are the same as the first figure, except the grenadier bag is made of black leather. The main difference with this unit is the grenadier caps with a brass forehead, with a monogram, coats of arms and armature (a sample from the collection of the Army Museum in Stockholm). The top of the cap was most likely a cloth in the shape of a "pod".

Grenadier (right) from the company of Captain Dannenfeld, the regiment of Delagardi (*Eständskt infanterieregemente*). A grenadier cap with a blue top "pod", a tassel made of red cloth. The royal coat of arms and grenades are embroidered on the red front plate, the embroidered grenades on the front red flap, and in the centrr are three azure leopard lions – the coat of arms of the province of Estland, and the cities of Revel (Tallinn). On the back flap five grenades, and below the yellow cord is inscribed "GRENADIRS DE DANNEN FELD".

Plate 5: Line infantry regiment: musician, pikeman, officer. For example Dal or Uppland regiments.

Drummer of the Life (*Leib*) Company of the Kroneborgsk (Kronoberg) infantry regiment, 1700. The hat and coat of the drummer are trimmed with yellow braid, and the drum sling is trimmed with a braid. The drum is painted. Ordinary company drums are painted in the colours of the regiment, with the image of the coat of arms of the regiment, or simply in flame-triangles. In this case, a motif repeats the banner of the company's flag and regimental banner, with the royal arms and the arms of the province in the right corner, in this case a red lion with a crossbow.

Pikeman of the infantry regiment (*Dal-regiment*), 1700. With the usual infantry uniform, blue with yellow lining, but buttons of yellow metal. As a headdress, the *karpus* cloth cap, blue with yellow flaps.

The officer (major) of the infantry regiment, a sample of the uniform and the version of his lacing is taken from the portrait of an officer of the Upplands regiment (Fleetwood, Georg Wilhelm.) The officer's sword belt is richly embroidered with gold stitching.

Plate 6: Line infantry regiment: pikeman, officer, musketeer. For example, Närke-Värmland or Nyland regiments.

Pikeman of Jönköpings regiment, 1700. A similar uniform was worn by the ranks of the Närke-Värmland regiment: blue, the lining and stocking also red. Camisole and breeches elk leather.

Officer of the Närke-Värmland regiment, 1700. Under the standard officer's uniform, the lining is in this case of a regimental, red colour.

Musketeer of the Nyland infantry regiment. The difference with this unit is the white colour of the lining of the uniform. The *karpus* cap is also blue and white, the flap trimmed along the edge with a blue-white cord, and in this style a sword knot is made also.

Plate 7: Line cavalry regiment: for example Nyland, Småland, Åbo & Björneborg counties' regiments.

Cavalryman of the Nyland and Tavastahas counties' regiment, 1700. The uniform in this regiment is made of grey undyed cloth with a red lining. Camisole and breeches elk skin. In 1700, the ranks of this regiment used cuirasses, either solely breastplates, or complete with the back plates. The Swedish cavalry was armed with new flintlock carbines, and they continued to use weapons with a wheellock, which was brought into combat readiness with a special key. The key was inserted into the pocket attached to the sword belt.

Cavalryman of the Åbo and Björneborg counties' regiment, 1701. The uniform and *karpus* of this regiment is completely grey, the rest of the armament and equipment is similar to the other regiments.

Cavalryman of the Småland Regiment (*Småland regemente*) 1700. The hat is trimmed with gold lace. The coat is blue with a yellow lining, with buttons of yellow metal.

Plate 8: Artillery: Officer, two 'other ranks'.

Artilleryman 1700, Narva. The gunner's uniform of this period was grey with blue lining, buttons of yellow metal. The *karpus* is grey with blue flaps, seams with a blue piping, and yellow braid. Camisole is elk skin with buttons of yellow metal, breeches also of elk. Blue stockings. On the sword belt, a special pattern of artillery cutlass with a brass grip.

Artillery officer 1700. In the hands of an officer, a measuring device. Officers of artillery also wore grey uniforms with a blue lining of different styles, including *justacorps*; loopholes could be lined with lace, stockings also blue. Officers were armed with swords and artillery cutlasses.

Artilleryman 1700 uniform similar to the first figure. Hat, linstock, wooden powder flask with brass plate with cipher. The belt for the cutlass was different from sword belts, as the cutlass hung vertically.

Bibliography

Most of the research about Sweden and the Great Northern War has, not surprisingly, been published in Swedish, although sometimes with summaries in English or some other major language.

Åberg, Alf; Göransson, Göte, *Karoliner* (*Caroleans*) (Stockholm: Trevi, 1976)

Åberg, Alf, *Fångars elände. Karolinerna i Ryssland 1700–1723* (*Prisoner's Misery. The Caroleans in Russia*) (Stockholm: Natur och kultur, 1991)

Aldridge, David Dennis, *Admiral Sir John Norris and the British Naval Expeditions to the Baltic Sea 1715–1727* (Lund: Nordic Academic Press, 2009)

Artéus, Gunnar, *Karolinsk och europeisk stridstaktik 1700–1712* (Carolean and European battle tactics 1700–1712) (Gothenburg: Historical Institute, 1972)

Englund, Peter, *The Battle that Shook Europe: Poltava and the Birth of the Russian Empire* (London: I.B. Tauris, 2013)

Eriksson, Peter, *Stora nordiska kriget förklarat. Karl XII och det ideologiska tilltalet* (*The Great Northern War. Charles XII and the ideological approach*) (Uppsala: Uppsala University, 2002)

Florén, Anders; Dahlgren, Stellan; Lindegren, Jan, *Kungar och krigare. Tre essäer om Karl X Gustav, Karl XI och Karl XII* (*Kings and warriors. Three essays about Charles X Gustavus, Charles XI and Charles XII*) (Stockholm: Atlantis, 1992)

From, Peter, *Katastrofen vid Poltava: Karl XII:s ryska fälttåg 1707–1709* (*The disaster at Poltava: Charles XII's Russian campaign 1707–1709*) (Lund: Historiska Media, 2007)

Frost, Robert, *The Northern Wars. War, State and Society in Northeastern Europe 1558–1721* (London, New York: Routledge, 2000)

Glete, Jan, *Swedish Naval Administration 1521–1721: Resource Flows and Organisational Capabilities* (Leiden: Brill, 2010)

Gudmundsson, David, *Konfessionell krigsmakt. Predikan och bön i den svenska armén 1611–1721* (*A confessional armed force. Sermon and prayer in the Swedish army 1611–1721*) (Lund: Malmö Universus Academic Press, 2014)

Hattendorf, John B. (ed.), *Charles XII: Warrior King* (forthcoming, Rotterdam 2018)

Hatton, Ragnhild M., *Charles XII of Sweden* (London: Weidenfeld and Nicolson, 1968)

Höglund, Lars-Eric; Sallnäs, Åke, *The Great Northern War 1700–1721. Colours and Uniforms* (Karlstad: Acedia Press, 2000)

Jonsson, Lena; Torstendahl Salytjeva, Tamara (eds.), *Poltava: krigsfångar och kulturutbyte* (*Poltava: Prisoners of War and cultural exchange*) (Stockholm: Atlantis, 2009; also publ. in Russian 2009)

King, Stephen L. (ed.), *Great Northern War Compendium. Volume One & Two* (St Louis: THGC Publishing, 2015)

Konstam, Angus, *Poltava* (Oxford: Osprey, 1994)

Konvaltjuk, Pavel; Lyth, Einar, *Vägen till Poltava. Slaget vid Lesnaja 1708* (*The Road to Poltava. The battle at Lesnaja 1708*) (Stockholm: Svenskt Militärhistorisk bibliotek, 2009)

Kronberg, Klas; Sandin, Per; Karlsson, Åsa (eds.), *When Sweden Was Ruled from the Ottoman Empire* (Stockholm: Armémuseum, 2016)

Kuvaja, Christer, *Försörjning av en ockupationsarmé. Den ryska arméns underhållssystem i Finland 1713–1721 (The supply of an occupation army. The maintenance system of the Russian army in Finland 1713–1721)* (Åbo: Åbo Akademis förlag, 1999)

Laidre, Margus, *Segern vid Narva. Början till en stormakts fall (The Battle at Narva. The Beginning of the Fall of a Great Power)* (Stockholm: Natur och kultur, 1996)

Laidre, Margus, *The Great Northern War and Estonia. The Trials of Dorpat 1700–1708* (Tallinn: Argo, 2010)

Larsson, Olle, *Stormaktens sista krig. Sverige och stora nordiska kriget 1700–1721 (The Last War of the Great Power. Sweden and the Great Northern War 1700–1721)* (Lund: Historiska Media, 2009)

Liljegren, Bengt, *Karl XII. En biografi (Charles XII. A Biography)* (Lund: Historiska Media, 2000)

Murray, John J., 'Robert Jackson's Mission to Sweden (1709–1717)', in *The Journal of Modern History*. Volume XXI:1, March 1949 pp 1–16

Oredsson, Sverker (ed.), *Tsar Peter och Kung Karl. Två härskare och deras folk (Tsar Peter and King Charles. Two Rulers and Their Peoples)* (Stockholm: Atlantis, 1998)

Roberts, Michael, ed., *Sweden's Age of Greatness 1632–1718* (London: Macmillan(?), 1973)

Roberts, Michael, *The Swedish Imperial Experience 1560–1718* (Cambridge: Cambridge University Press, 1979)

Roberts, Michael, *From Oxenstierna to Charles XII. Four Studies* (Cambridge: Cambridge University Press, 1991)

Sandin, Per (ed.), *Peter den store och Karl XII i krig och fred. Katalog för Livrustkammaren, Stockholm och Statliga Eremitaget, S:t Petersburg (Peter the Great and Charles XII in War and Peace. Catalogue for the Royal Armoury, Stockholm and the State Hermitage, St Petersburg)* (Stockholm: Livrustkammaren, 1998)

Sjöström, Oscar, *Fraustadt 1706 – ett fält färgat rött (A Field Dyed Red)* (Lund: Historiska Media, 2009)

Sundberg, Ulf, *Swedish Defensive Fortress Warfare in the Great Northern War 1702–1710* (Åbo/Turku 2018)

Tessin, Georg, *Die Deutschen Regimenter der Krone Schweden. Teil II, under Karl XI. und Karl XII. (1660–1718), (The German Regiments of the Swedish Crown. Part II, during Charles XI and Charles XII, (1660–1718))* (Köln, Graz: Böhlau, 1967)

Törnquist, Leif, 'Från banér till kommandotecken. En översikt över de svenska och finska fanorna och standaren genom tiderna', i *Meddelande XXXVIII*. Armémuseum 1977–78 ('From Banner to Command Flag. An Overview of the Swedish and Finnish Banners and Standards Through the Ages', in *Message XXXVIII*. Army Museum 1977–78) (Stockholm 1978 pp.7–158)

Ullgren, Peter, *Det stora nordiska kriget 1700–1721. En berättelse om stormakten Sveriges fall (The Great Northern War 1700–1721. A Story of the Fall of the Great Power of Sweden)* (Stockholm: Prisma, 2008)

Waxberg, Henry, *Hästen i det karolinska rytteriet. Studier i det indelta rytteriets hästhållning (The Horse in the Carolean Cavalry. Studies in the Horse Keeping in the Allotted Cavalry)* (Stockholm: LT, 1973)

Wolke, Lars Ericson, *Svenska knektar. Indelta soldater, ryttare och båtsmän i krig och fred (Swedish Soldiers. Alloted Soldiers, Cavalrymen and sailors in war and peace)* (Lund: Historiska Media, 1995 and later editions)

Wolke, Lars Ericson, et al., *Svenska slagfält (Swedish battlefields)* (Stockholm: Wahlström & Widstrand, 2003)

Wolke, Lars Ericson, *Sjöslag och rysshärjningar. Kampen om Östersjön under stora nordiska kriget 1700–1721* (*Sea Battles and Russian Ravages. The Struggle for the Baltic Sea During the Great Northern War*) (Stockholm: Norstedts, 2012)

An impressive amount of information about organisation and equipment details have been researched and published by Hans Högman: www.hhogman.se. His webpage is also published in an English version.

A large number of important studies have been published in *Karolinska Förbundets Årsbok* (*The yearbook of the Carolean Society*), which has been published since 1910.